TIME WILL SAY NOTHING

TIME WILL
SAY NOTHING

RAMIN JAHANBEGLOO

Printed and bound in Canada at Friesens.

Library and Archives Canada Cataloguing in Publication
Cataloguing in Publication (CIP) data available at the Library and
Archives Canada web site: www.collectionscanada.gc.ca and at
www.uofrpress.ca/publications/Time-Will-Say-Nothing

University of Regina Press
Saskatchewan, Canada, S4S 0A2
tel: (306) 585-4758   fax: (306) 585-4699
web: www.uofrpress.ca

10   9   8   7   6   5   4   3   2   1

The University of Regina Press acknowledges the financial support
of the following for its publishing program and activities: a Creative
Saskatchewan Production Grant, and the Creative Industry Growth and
Sustainability program, both made possible through funding provided to
the Saskatchewan Arts Board by the Government of Saskatchewan through
the Ministry of Parks, Culture, and Sport; the Government of Canada
through the Canada Book Fund; and the Canada Council for the Arts.

To my mother, Khoji,
who has been my consolation in sorrow
and my strength in weakness

Time will say nothing but I told you so,
Time only knows the price we have to pay;
If I could tell you I would let you know.

—W.H. AUDEN

Preface

OUR DESTINIES ARE UNIQUE, EACH IN ITS OWN WAY.
Each of us is a creator, shaping and reshaping ourselves
to become what we are, as life ultimately means taking
one's destiny and imbuing it with meaning. That is what
makes destiny a moral dilemma. In Hindu philosophy,
which incorporates a belief in reincarnation, destiny is
both passed to us at birth and shaped by us in our new
life, out of our free will. We all wear the chains we forge
in life, but while some of us try to break our chains and
set ourselves free, others stay in fetters. As Goethe says,
"There is no predicament that we cannot ennoble either
by doing or enduring." There are moments in life when
we must re-engage with truth, especially in the face of
horror. Perhaps this engagement is an attempt to awaken
memories of the past, moments of joy and pain. Extreme
situations and intense suffering help us to piece together

fragments of memory. Dreams and nightmares are tinged with painful secrets, losses, betrayals, but also with kindness and love.

A man awakens in a prison cell with no memory of his past. He thinks of dying as the best thing that could happen to him. And yet he continues to live under the shadow of his destiny, because he has the chance to walk away from his past and create the future he always wanted. This is the story of my struggle with destiny.

1

THE HEAVY STEEL DOOR SWUNG CLOSED ON THE cell behind me. In the total silence that descended, I took off my blindfold and found myself trapped within four cold walls. I looked around, my eyes adjusting, as if emerging from a dream, as if waking into a nightmare. The cell was small, perhaps three by three metres. A high ceiling and old concrete. All green. An intense yellow light from a single bulb high above. There were two blankets on the floor next to a small vent set in the wall. Somehow I could hear the horror in the walls, the voices of previous prisoners whispering a painful welcome. I could see the traces they had left on the walls, despite the green paint that was supposed to cover the signs of their distress. I had no way of knowing whether they had survived the time they spent here. I had no way of knowing whether I would. Even if I lived, would I be able to survive solitary confinement without going insane? So many questions were crowding my mind. I was isolated and disoriented. I heard my own breathing and then, as if from a great distance, the sound of a man moaning. It was coming through the vent. Later, I found out that he was so injured that he could barely move. He had to be helped by the guards to go to the bathroom. I realized that he must have been tortured. Would I be tortured too?

I was afraid. The cell had the look, the sound, the desolate feel of Carl Theodor Dreyer's film *Vampyr*, and I had been thrown into it without any warning. Why? How had I gotten here? I lay down on the blankets on the hard floor and the images and sounds of the past hour came rushing back, furious and absurd.

It was the morning of April 27, 2006, and I was at Tehran's Mehrabad Airport to catch a flight to Brussels, where I was to attend a conference. I had checked in my luggage and gone through security when I was approached by four men. One of them called me by my first name. "Ramin," he said, "could you follow us?"

I looked them over quickly. They were all wearing ordinary suits with no ties and had beards. Two of them were particularly ugly and rough, reminding me of unkempt wrestlers. The one who had spoken looked the most boorish, and he stood impatiently, waiting for me to comply.

"I'll miss my plane," I said.

"We just want to ask you a few questions."

People around us were watching, but nobody moved. I realized that I had no choice but to go with them.

They led me to the lower, arrivals, level, and soon we were outside by the shuttle buses. One of them told me, as we got into a waiting car, that my luggage would be safe—it was the last thing on my mind, but his words were still strangely reassuring. Two of the men got in the front as driver and passenger, and the other two climbed in the back with me between them. They pushed my head down and the car took off toward another part of the airport, to a garage where another car was waiting.

Here, with fewer witnesses around, the men were more aggressive, pulling me out of the first car and throwing me into the second. They pushed my head down again and this time one of them covered it with his jacket, which smelled of rotten onions. It had a hole in it, so that I could see out of one of the side windows. The car sped away from the airport and I soon saw that we were getting on the highway, heading for northern Tehran. Then I heard one of them say into a walkie-talkie: "We have the package. The package is arriving."

I realized for the first time that my life was in danger. I knew that in the early years of the Islamic regime many people had been taken away and executed without notice or trial. Their mutilated bodies were found in the suburbs, and the police pretended to look for the assassins.

Their abductors were similar to the men surrounding me—intelligence officers who picked up intellectuals and activists and killed them on the spot. Two days earlier I had returned to Iran, which apparently had not changed. In a place that a lifetime of studying philosophy cannot explain, no amount of thinking could help me. Instinct prevailed and I panicked. An agitated voice kept escaping me, though I was not aware of speaking. It echoed, bouncing around the car, falling back into my throat and escaping again. "Where are you taking me? Where are you taking me?" And the simple, hollow reply, "Shut up!" over and over again.

I had never thought that I would be relieved to approach the grim walls of Evin Prison, but relief is exactly what I felt when I recognized, through the hole in the jacket, a square in the Saadat Abad neighbourhood near the infamous prison. I knew then that I would not be murdered, at least not immediately. A few minutes later, the car drove through the first gate into the prison. When we stopped at the second gate, I heard the driver present his identification card and say, "We have a package for 209." I later learned that 209 is a section of Evin Prison administered by the Ministry of Intelligence, an interrogation centre that no one, not even members of the government, can enter or leave without a permit. I couldn't see the prison as we drove into it, but I knew that I had arrived at my final destination. I felt paralyzed.

Hands grabbed me and I was blindfolded and taken inside the main gate. There was, of course, no arrest procedure—no fingerprints taken, no phone call allowed. It was brutally simple: they led me by the arm from one room to the next, and I heard one of them say that we were going to the administration room. When we arrived there, I heard someone else say, "Where are his belongings? Go and bring a prison uniform for him." A few minutes later, I was told to take off my clothes and put on the uniform. I couldn't see it, but it felt like polyester pyjamas. Then they told me to sit down. I felt a hand on my shoulder and a voice said, with unforgettable ominousness, "This is the last stop." The menace in the voice was horrifying. I felt cold sweat on my back. For a few seconds I thought "the last stop" meant my meaningless death. I was absolutely afraid, which is difficult to describe in words. Terror is more excruciating than the most dreadful death you can imagine.

Section 209 is the last stop before hell—a horrifying place to spend even a little time. It is the autonomous realm of Iranian security officers and interrogators who are free to do whatever they wish with their prisoners. In their view, the inmates of Section 209 are spies, traitors, enemies of Islam or the Iranian Revolution who deserve to be humiliated and abused. Those who are not well-known are dumped into solitary cells without any medical attention and ignored by prison staff.

Iran has a long history of tyrannies, cruelties, and violence. For centuries philosophers, poets, and reformers have been jailed, tortured, and killed for daring to think or act in ways that contradict the official line of thought. Even those who did not talk or act against their kings or leaders have been thrown into dungeons because they refused to agree with them. Iranian prisons have always functioned as institutions of sheer terror, and their purpose is the negation of the individual. This is especially true in the current era of Iranian history. Since the Shah's time, "Evin" has been a synonym for torture, execution, and suffering. The Iranian Revolution in 1979 did not put an end to this dreadful place of suffering and death. On the contrary, Iran's new leaders, believing that violence was necessary to achieve liberation in the name of God, thought that Evin Prison was the perfect school for those who wanted to confess their sins—or for those who were destined to suffer and die without knowing what sin they had committed. If the revolution was necessary, if terror was necessary, then Evin Prison was also necessary.

But why was I here? I was, and am, a scholar of philosophy, an academic. But history shows us that no revolution tolerates philosophers and poets, even those who support it. Stalin loathed Mandelstam, Akhmatova, and Pasternak; Franco abhorred Lorca; and Pinochet assassinated Victor Jara. There was no reason the Iranian Revolution would tolerate someone like me, though I was not a poet and my philosophical writings and teachings did not preach any form of violence. I suppose one reason that Iran's revolutionaries hated me is that I didn't hate the Revolution—I simply didn't find it necessary any longer, although I had been passionate about it when I was in my early twenties. But now I was sitting, blindfolded, in a room with my captors, asking myself why I'd been caught in this Dante's *Inferno*.

Life had not been easy for intellectuals, artists, journalists, and human rights activists since the election of President Mahmoud Ahmadinejad in 2005, and many had been arrested. I knew that as a thinker on the margin of Iranian society, I was not safe and so, rather than stay in Iran, I had accepted a job offer in Delhi. I had come back to Tehran for my summer vacation and only two days later was arrested at the airport on my way to a conference. But why? Why me and why now? Why at the airport and not at my home? I supposed they didn't want my family to be there when they arrested me. Also, this was probably the best time for them to build a case against me. No one inside the regime would support me and no one in civil society would dare to back me.

Suddenly I felt someone take my hand. "Follow me!" he said.

"Where are you taking me?"

"Not a word, you understand? Just follow me . . ."

I couldn't see his face, but I could smell the stench of his sweat. I counted twelve paces and then we climbed up some stairs. I was handed to another guard, who had an Azeri accent. He too sounded tired and frustrated. He took my hand roughly, guided me to a closed solid steel door, and unlocked it. I took off my blindfold and stepped into the cell that became my home for the next fifty days, until I was transferred to another, a little bigger.

2

I WAS SITTING ON THE FLOOR OF MY CELL, LOOKING at the blindfold in my hands. The absolute silence surrounding me was frightening. I felt as if I were the only human being trapped in this dungeon, although I knew that could not be the case. I knew that there were many prisoners in Evin Prison. But I was not supposed to see them or hear them. Feeling as if I was living among ghosts, I looked around the room. The walls had been newly painted to erase the traces of previous lives, but there were still signs of a few words. I managed to read "Dey 1384" (December 2005). Other prisoners had been here before me. God knows what had happened to them. Had they been tortured? Executed? Freed? Would I also be freed? Maybe tomorrow or the day after? They must know that I was not a political activist, and I hoped I was there for a simple interrogation.

These questions went around and around in my mind while I played with the blindfold in my hands. I was suddenly flooded with memories from almost forty years earlier—memories of playing hide-and-seek with boys from my neighbourhood. It is surprising how a scrap of cloth, a terrifying blindfold, can bring back sensations from the past. Our lives are not measured by the number of sensations we have but by the moments that give rise to those sensations. I closed my eyes. My heart started to beat faster. I breathed in. I am eleven years old and I am back in our old house in North Tehran with its huge garden where we used to keep sheep, hens, roosters, ducks, geese, cats, and dogs. I am playing.

The boys who joined me in the game were the son of a taxi driver and the son of an American military officer. We played together happily, indifferent to history and unaware of the cultural and political barriers that divided our parents and nations. Kids are ignorant of the mental ghettos that make adults hate and kill each other. Our sacred adolescent world was devoid of gods, filled instead with heroes, characters like Robin Hood, Tarzan, and Tom Sawyer. I read everything I could on the tales of Robin and his band of Merry Men and watched the movie with Errol Flynn at least fifteen times, but Tom Sawyer was my favourite hero. Whenever I reread *Tom Sawyer*, which I still do from time to time, it takes me back to my childhood. *Tom Sawyer* is a quintessentially American novel, but Tom's character is universal. That is why an adolescent like me in the Iran of the 1960s could easily relate to the adventures of a boy growing up in a Mississippi River town in the early nineteenth century. I was not a mischievous boy like Tom but, like him, I envied Huck Finn's lazy lifestyle and freedom. I transposed Tom's unflagging energy and thirst for adventure to my Iranian garden, sharing my Twainian escapades with my cousin, who personified Huck. We spent the long, hot summer days hunting for treasure in our garden and pretending an ugly peddler was Injun Joe. These are sweet memories of my happy and secure childhood.

I grew up in a largely traditional world, which insisted that children act like small-scale adults. But the character of Tom Sawyer let me act out my fantasies of adventure and heroism. It is not for nothing that Twain called his novel a "hymn to childhood." Despite all the years that separate me from the Iranian adventures of Tom and Huck, I retain the memory of a perfect innocence, of the fears, joy, triumphs, and hopes of a child. Memory is a way of travelling, not a destination, as is imagination. I travelled in my imagination as a child. It took me thousands of miles out onto the oceans and up into the mountains. What it showed existed, was real, was possible.

During my first hours in my tiny cell, I drifted in and out of such visions. I had no sense of time. The light in the ceiling was permanently lit, so I could not distinguish day from night. My childhood memories circled through my mind in a meaningless dance.

It was 1973. I was sixteen and in grade 11 at Iran-zamin Tehran International School. This was the year of the Watergate scandal and General Augusto Pinochet's coup d'état against President Salvador Allende's govern-ment in Chile. It was the year Pink Floyd's album *The Dark Side of the Moon* was released. The school held a monthly dance, and that month, as a senior member of the International Club, I was in charge of selling tickets at the front door. One of my classmates, Farshid, who wore glasses and looked a bit like Woody Allen, asked me if he could go out for a minute. I made the mistake of letting him go and paid the price for it. He came back with a bottle of Iranian vodka tucked under his vest. He showed it to me as a sign of his adulthood, as teenagers do when they smoke or talk dirty. I let him go and he disappeared in the main building. An hour later, around 9:00 p.m., I went down on the dance floor, where some of my classmates and other kids from the school were dancing to a track on Santana's album *Abraxas*. I noticed Farshid moving strangely. I asked two of my other class-mates, Hamid and Ali, if everything was all right and they said that they were worried about Farshid. They had joined him in drinking the vodka, but they were both still sober. I asked them to help me take Farshid outside into the school garden before one of the teachers found out about the vodka. They agreed, and we got him out through a back window without anyone realizing what was going on.

Farshid was in bad shape and started vomiting down the front of my shirt. I took off my shirt and washed it under a hose, while my friends hid him from our chaperones. But it was already too late. One of the teachers found us and told the vice-principal. Farshid had passed out, and the vice-principal called his father. By the time he arrived we were ready to take Farshid to a poison treatment centre at Tehran Hospital for Sick Children, twenty minutes away by car.

I could not believe what I saw there. It was chaos in the emergency bloc. There was a drunk in a torn shirt and dirty trousers who had been brought in by a police officer, a drug addict who, tied by his hands to a bed, was hallucinating, and a small kid who was being prepared to have his stomach pumped. The two of us who had accompanied Farshid's father had to wait in the corridor, but I could see through the screen on the window how my friend was treated. The nurse fed a tube through Farshid's mouth and poured what I later learned was potassium permanganate down the tube three times. Each time Farshid threw up like a volcano erupting. Then the nurse gave him a serum and he was wheeled off to another room.

His father asked us to leave because there was nothing more we could do. It was already near midnight. I knew the front door to my house would be locked and I would have to wake up my parents to get in. My friend, who was being driven by his chauffeur, offered me a ride. It was nearly 1:00 a.m. when I arrived home. Fearful of being scolded by my parents, I decided not to ring the doorbell but to jump over one of the low walls around our garden. Once in the garden, I saw a dim light on the terrace. My parents were awake and worried. They had called the school and learned what had happened. I told them my version of the story and went to bed. My shirt was still wet and I was exhausted by the whole adventure.

The next day, a school holiday, I gave my parents more details about the event and they didn't seem worried. On Saturday I went to school as usual. I had barely arrived in my classroom when I was told to go to the principal's office. The principal was an American, Mr. Irvine, and the vice-principal, Mrs. Sahakian, was an Armenian woman in her fifties who terrified us kids. I wondered why I had to go to the principal's office so early in the morning but soon had my answer. Farshid, Hamid, Ali, and another friend were standing in the middle of the room and Mrs. Sahakian was bombarding them with questions. Farshid was evidently feeling much better and gave me a look of thanks from behind his glasses. I thought a smile would be the right response. I was wrong.

"Take that smile off your face," Mrs. Sahakian said. "Tell me, did you know that drinking is forbidden in this school?"

"Yes, I know, Madam," I replied.

"So, why didn't you inform the chaperones when you learned that he"—she pointed to Farshid—"brought a bottle of vodka into the dance party?"

"I suppose I did wrongly, Madam." I was terrified.

"You suppose? You suppose! Well, I'll have nothing to do with your suppositions. You and these gentlemen are expelled from school for a week. Go and get your stuff from your lockers. One of the janitors will take you home with a note to your parents from me."

And that was it. On a sunny day of November 1973, while the world was following the evil actions of Augusto Pinochet and the sinful lies of Richard Nixon, I was expelled from school because I was guilty of neither lying nor being a snitch. The story, however, had a happy ending. My parents fully supported me and all three of us were quickly reinstated in school. Now, thirty-three years later, I was in Evin Prison, presumably because in my writings on nonviolence I had refused to lie to my conscience or to others.

SOME TIME LATER I drifted into a dream, and was startled awake by a voice shouting, "Wake up, wake up." It wasn't the voice of my father, who used to wake me every day by shaking my feet with his strong, gentle hand. It was the raspy voice of a prison guard standing in the doorway. "Get ready for the interrogation," he said.

3

I WAS BLINDFOLDED, THE HEAVY STEEL DOOR CLOSED behind me, and I was led by the hand through cold corridors, up and down stairs, past what I assumed were other cells and other barred doors. Through a tiny gap at the bottom of the blindfold I could see the ground beneath my feet, which was slightly comforting, and, strangely, I could hear birds singing. Later I was told by one the guards that these were canaries kept to cover the noise of interrogations; they were taken care of by one of the prisoners, just like Robert Stroud, the Birdman of Alcatraz.

As I walked to the interrogation room, I couldn't help but think of Josef K., the central character in Franz Kafka's *The Trial,* a novel that foreshadowed the fate of countless political prisoners and intellectual activists in the twentieth century and beyond. Like Josef K., I had been arrested and taken away without being told why; incriminated without knowing what crime I had committed.

Josef K. is lost from the beginning, doomed to wander through a cold, irrational world as the unseen hands of bureaucracy and tyranny slowly tighten their grip, crushing him. The way Kafka describes the offices of the court—in disrepair and stifling—indicates how arbitrary and unfathomable the system is. Yet the most terrifying thing about K.'s fate is that everything unfolds with chilly efficiency and almost logical consistency. He constantly vacillates between hope and anxiety, as the world around him vacillates between order and chaos.

After K. is arrested, he is told that an inquiry into his case will be conducted, following regular procedure. His accusers seem thoughtful and considerate, quite reasonable. But under their deliberations lies madness: his crime is never made clear, and he is broken without ever learning why. Kafka's mysterious courts and absurd laws are frighteningly similar to Iran's legal system today. The violence of this absurd system is demonstrated not only by the resulting injustice but also by the fact that the law affects every aspect of society; there is no escaping it.

What Kafka shows us is that the concept of innocence is of no importance in a world where the goal is the alienation of the individual from the rest of society. As the prison chaplain says in the story, "It is not necessary to accept everything as true, one must only accept it as necessary." What is necessary is to accept being guilty without knowing what one has done. I had to acknowledge this absurdity when I was led into one of the interrogation rooms in Evin Prison, where I was to meet my three perfectly reasonable inquisitors, the men whose aim was to break me. From that moment on, guilt became the painful companion of my innocence.

I was taken into a concrete room lined with sound-proofing. I was still blindfolded, but I could smell the rotten cork they'd used to cover the walls. I was ordered to sit on a hard chair facing the wall at the far end of the room. Then I waited. After what seemed like hours I heard footsteps behind me. It sounded as if two men had entered. But they said nothing and seemed to be waiting for something else to happen. I could hear the sound of their breathing, then I heard the low mumble of voices. I held my breath and waited. Eventually a third man came in, sat down behind me; he was the first to talk to me.

"Oh, very interesting. Mr. Jahanbegloo, the great intellectual, is here," he said. "What are you doing here in prison?"

"I think there has been a mistake," I said immediately.

"No, no, there is no mistake," he said drily. "You have been brought here because you are accused of a conspiracy.

against the Iranian state. You are implicated in a *baran-dazi narm*."

I had never heard these words before. The direct translation from Farsi would be a "soft overthrow." Later I decided that what he meant by that is known in English as a velvet revolution. But at the time I asked him, in my confusion, to clarify what he meant.

"You know better than I what a soft overthrow is," he said.

The thread of a normal conversation was already slipping away. I realized that there would be no rational basis to our discussions. These men were not trained in political theory or in law. Their only skill was the ability to intimidate, through either senseless rhetoric or aggression.

I never learned their real names and at first I identified them only by their shoes, the only thing I could see from under the blindfold while they walked around me. The principal interrogator, the man who had spoken, wore old brown dress shoes with no laces, flattened at the back in the Persian way. Later, the others would refer to him as Hajj Agha, which, literally, is a title used for someone who has made the pilgrimage to Mecca, but the interrogators used it for each other as a sign of their fidelity to Islam. Hajj Agha claimed to be a university professor, but, though he used the word "methodology" frequently, he never showed any sign of having had a humanist education. The other two were much more reticent and served as echoes of the chief officer. Their pseudonyms were Hajj Ali and Hajj Saeed, and judging by their shoes, I could tell why they were minor characters. The first wore a pair of ragged running shoes; the second household sandals. Despite my disgust, I often stared at the hairy feet these revealed, with their toenails all bent out of shape, feeling that they would somehow give me insight into his personality. Once when I was looking at his feet, he dropped a nail clipper and a small pocket English dictionary, which landed neatly beside them. This incongruous detail heightened the ludicrousness of the situation. It was as if this place were his home, where he harassed and tortured people as part of his daily chores. Later, this man, Saeed, and his colleague in the running shoes would play the role of the "good cops," trying to endear themselves to me, using softer interrogation techniques. But whenever they lost patience and became angry with me for refusing to co-operate, they would turn into ruthless villains, men who did not hesitate to threaten me and my family.

In this first interrogation, though, everything was still unclear to me, even though it was gradually and awkwardly unfolded by Hajj Agha. When I told him that I still could not understand what I was supposed to be implicated in and what they wanted from me, he proceeded to lay out a conspiracy theory, which they must have spent a lot of time constructing, though in the end it was nothing but a web of nonsense.

"You see, Mr. Jahanbegloo, we know for a fact for whom you are working. We've been through your emails. We have two rooms full of documents, with video clips and writings, newspaper cuttings, and voice recordings on you and all that you have done with your life. It all testifies to your guilt. So you're better off telling us from the beginning what your role is in this soft overthrow and giving us the details of how your employers instructed you to carry it out."

"What employers? What are you talking about?"

Hajj Agha exhaled his cigarette smoke slowly, patiently, and I felt it enveloping me from behind like a fog of uncertainty.

"The United States and Israel, of course. Do you think we're stupid? We know you've been meeting with American and Israeli scholars, with politicians, with activists. You've done it all out in the open. There are video recordings of your meetings with them, countless articles and books that you've collaborated on with them. Shall I go on? You know best what role you've played in working with them, and that your intention has been to change the government of the Islamic Republic to better suit their interests."

What could I say? If you looked at my writings to see what I had been doing for the previous twenty years, you'd soon realize that I talk only about nonviolent change and reform. My interrogators would say that nonviolent reform is the same thing as a velvet revolution, but for me there was a distinction. How could I convince these men that I was innocent; that what they had interpreted as wrongdoing was merely my wish to see my country do better, to treat its citizens with respect and dignity, to show that reform did not necessitate a complete change of government or a swing toward subservience and the foreign domination we had endured in the past? No, to men like these, who had swallowed the revolutionary ideology of the Islamic Republic, there was no talking sense. Trying to do so would be confronting absurdity in human form. I was already guilty in their eyes, and they already knew what I was guilty of. In a way, my innocence was working against me, because what in a normal society is supposed to define you as a decent man is an anomaly in a place like the Islamic Republic of Iran.

There was nothing to say. I could only respond to their questions with shorter questions that clarified nothing. Our language game, with all the rules in disarray, frightened me. The interrogation had turned into a life or death struggle, which constantly drew near to madness. Fearing death, I experienced the dissolution of my freedom, the melting-away of my being, but at the same time I knew that I was discovering the very truth of my self-consciousness. It became clear that fear of death is a strong vehicle for the self-revelation of the truth of self-consciousness. In a sense, the absolute negativity of death became a crucial premise that allowed me to recognize myself as a person freed from his frozen instincts. Ultimately, confinement led to the appropriation of death and a transformation of it into a new existential experience.

In the days that followed, Hajj Ali would arrive at Evin Prison early each afternoon and ask the guards to take me out of my cell. He had made it his job to make a good Muslim out of me. Each time, once we were alone, he would tell me to remove my blindfold and to sit next to him on a carpet on the floor. And each time the conversation would revolve around religion and the fact that I had lost my faith in Islam. Once he looked me in the eyes and asked, "Do you consider yourself to be a true Muslim?"

"What exactly do you mean?" I said.

"Do you know the names of the twelve Shiite Imams?" he barked.

"Yes, I do. Ali ibn Abu Talib, Hasan ibn Ali, Husayn ibn Ali, Zayn al-Abidin—"

"Enough. I am sure you don't know how to pray," he said.

"My grandmother taught me how to pray when I was twelve, but—" I was trying to find an answer to get out of his trap. He cut me off.

"No wonder you became a spy. You come from a family of non-believers. Is it true that your father was a communist?"

"My father was an idealist, and his great ideal was to change himself and to enrich the world."

"But he failed and went to prison. In the same way that you failed because you made the wrong choices in life."

My inner voice was murmuring, "Did I make the wrong choices? Perhaps, because I was born in a time when people have no respect for anything. But I did not choose to be born in the twentieth century. I chose neither my parents nor my country. They chose me."

I got back to him with a little more confidence: "We usually make a living by what we get but we can make a life out of what we wish."

He stood up in a fury. "Stop philosophizing. We are not in a classroom and I am not your student. I am not here to listen to you. You have to listen to me. If I have to, I will make sure that you are kept in this cell for years. Then you would not get to see your daughter. I want to try and save you in spite of yourself, but you need to collaborate with us."

I couldn't look at him. Birds of fear were flying around inside my head. I was shocked and terribly angry. I fixed my eyes on the carpet, which seemed to set the tone of our conversation. Its busy, machine-made pattern was neither warm nor relaxing but it served to hide stains and encourage prisoners to look at their interrogators instead of looking down.

Finally I asked, "What do you mean by collaboration? I have never collaborated with any government. I am not interested in power."

"But power is beautiful when it is on the side of God. We are servants of Islam and Iran," he said.

"I always thought that you cannot serve God and politics at the same time. You can't serve two masters," I said.

"Well, I serve the Guide of the Revolution and his will is that of God."

There was no way I could argue with him. My precarious political situation as a prisoner made it impossible. I just nodded.

"You have to collaborate. You have to confess," he continued. And then he dialled a number on his cellphone and started talking to another person about a business plan he had. I didn't listen to the phone conversation. I was still thinking of his words "collaborate" and "confess," which had hit me like rocks. For the first time in my life someone was asking me to confess something.

What was I supposed to confess? I hadn't committed any crime and didn't think of myself as guilty of anything. Deep down I was shivering with rage. The fear of being thought superfluous was killing me. Should I confess like the former Bolshevik leader Nikolai Bukharin did after he was arrested in 1937? Why he confessed is no mystery: Arthur Koestler reveals it in his novel *Darkness at Noon*. The main character, Rubashov, confesses because of his commitment to protecting communism. I had no ideology to protect, but I had to protect my mother, my wife, and my daughter. My family did not know where I was, and I had no right to an attorney or counsel. Bukharin held out for three months against the Stalinist threats inside prison, but he finally confessed after the investigators threatened to kill his wife and newborn son. Who was I to be stronger than Bukharin? I was not indebted to history or to the Revolution.

Many people are unaware that confessions are obtained by the use of threats and psychological torture. Their purpose is to confirm a conspiracy theory. The fear of conspiracy promotes the use of violence against perceived conspirators. Terror generates accusations. Accusations escalate into more threats and more violence. And threats produce more confessions and yet more accusations. It is a vicious circle, a huge, terrible wheel powered by insane people in power.

Hajj Ali ended his phone call. He looked at me and must have realized that I was deeply tortured by my thoughts.

"Think of what I told you. Put your blindfold back on." He called one of the guards by his number. "Number 430, come here and take the prisoner back to his cell."

4

WHEN MY INTERROGATORS FIRST ACCUSED ME OF
preparing a velvet revolution in Iran, I thought it was an
absurd joke. The level of its absurdity appeared to be equal
to the absence of political knowledge on the part of my
jail keepers. But it was a way for them to portray me as a
spy intent on betraying the Great Islamic Revolution in
Iran. One day I was cast as a CIA agent, the next a James
Bond-type spy, and the third day a dirty Zionist with a
Canadian passport. At almost every interrogation I was
accused of being a shameless enemy of the Islamic Revolution. It is true that I do not care much about revolutions, so my conscience was clear and clean. My passion
for individual freedom and democratic rule, as well as my
deep respect for the political struggle of Eastern Euro-
peans against the Soviet system and my friendship with
anti-totalitarian intellectuals like Václav Havel, Adam

Michnik, and Agnes Heller, never made me think of the Czech, Polish, and Hungarian anti-communist revolutions as appropriate models for the future of Iran. Each nation has its own spiritual identity and its political actors must follow it. Iran is not a Catholic country like Poland or a Protestant society like the Czech Republic. It is a curious mixture of ontological, anthropological, and political layers: a pre-Islamic nationalist pride, a Shiite fatalist view of the world, and a modern hedonistic individualism. Iranians are heirs to three modes of thought: Pre-Islamic Persian, Islamic, and Western. For them, affirmation of the Perso-Islamic heritage and the acquisition of Western knowledge are both considered ways to protect one's identity. Nothing can move ahead in this country without the contribution of at least one of these factors. One way or another, it is out of this shared identity that the meaning and content of our liberty as Iranians will ultimately emerge.

This meaning is by no means a megalomaniacal feeling that we Iranians are better than all the rest. On the contrary, it should make us permanently conscious of our historical shortcomings. Clearly, it is the role of intellectuals to think far ahead of the pack, but it is not a good idea for them to underestimate the metaphysical inclinations of the people. Absolute radicalism has never been the best way to political success and national glory in any country, especially Iran. That is why the ability to judge whether we can take an inspiring step forward toward significant change through nonviolent resistance is not the sole property of radicalism. It is a morally grounded responsibility.

Sometimes people say that I am too much of a philosopher or an idealist when I assert this. But I think this sense of moral responsibility stems from my personal conviction against endorsing closed and dogmatic doctrines. I learned from living in Iran and Europe to think independently, using my power of critical reasoning. I have not always been right, but my mistakes have been the fruits of my intellectual shortcomings rather than of any political or religious inclinations. Most of all, I have never been attracted to any kind of political power or ideology, either of the left or the right. I refuse to categorize myself as a liberal or a radical. For me the greatest form of radicalism is that of the intellect and the best use of a liberal temperament is the support of civil liberties even against neo-liberal rule. In short, I become deeply wary whenever I feel the weight of fanaticism. And, suddenly, in the interrogation rooms of the Evin Prison, I found myself under the constant pressure of the worst form of religious fanaticism. I will never forget the ugly hatred, the lies and suspicions that filled the air each time I was taken blindfolded to an interrogation room. But you do

not need to go to prison in Iran to become aware that
Iranian politics has mobilized the worst human qualities:
egoism, envy, hatred, and incivility.

Many of us Iranians deserve what we get, because
the Revolution is responsible for what we have become
and we are responsible for the Revolution. Every generation lives its own revolution as well as the revolution
of its ancestors. We made a revolution to show our Persianness to the world and now we are insisting on our
Persianness to get rid of a revolution. Iranians are the
mirror of their history, though many say and feel the
opposite, and the best way to introduce change in us is
to encourage the true understanding of our own history.
As Cicero says, "To be ignorant of what occurred before
you were born is to remain always a child." However, it is
often difficult for nations to transcend their immaturity.
Kant defines immaturity as the inability to use one's own
understanding without the guidance of another. However,
he believes that the public use of reason alone can bring
about enlightenment. In the past 150 years some Iranian
intellectuals, like the German thinkers of the eighteen
and nineteenth centuries, have tried to turn universities
into centres of the Enlightenment. Some proposed that
this Enlightenment could be implemented by modern
despots, such as Reza Shah and Mohammad Reza Shah
Pahlavi, rulers who imposed reform by authoritarian

means. Others advocated revolutionary means, perhaps following the example of Che Guevara and using guerilla warfare, while others chose French-style salons and other forms of public intervention as the new venues for new ideas. But most of these Iranian intellectuals came from the elite of society and had little connection with ordinary people; Iranian politics prior to the Revolution was, in effect, a politics of the salons because its power was massively curtailed by the Shah. People were too afraid to discuss politics outside their homes. Perhaps because of this fear, politics during the Shah's regime was more a matter of heroic action than an art of managing society. Most Iranian intellectuals of that time—and still today—who enjoy popular appeal find themselves in exile or sidelined, removed from the Iranian public sphere. Nevertheless, many young Iranians, inspired by what has been called an Iranian renaissance, believe in the liberating principles of democracy and secularism. The day Iran is truly democratic, Iranian intellectuals will put less effort into fighting for the idea of democracy and for liberal values. That sounds like a tautology, but in a way we are more empowered by the struggle to attain democracy than we will be by its existence. Today, even in the West, democracy is more a matter of dissent than of institutions and regulations that kill the spirit of change. Martin Luther King Jr. once said:

"Democracy transformed from thin paper to thick action is the greatest form of government on earth." If Americans and Canadians had continued to read people like Martin Luther King Jr., their societies would have been very different. The tragedy is that Canadian democracy has remained with thin paper, without moving towards thick action.

For the time being, we are in a Sartrian situation. Sartre starts his essay "The Republic of Silence" in a very provocative manner, saying, "We were never more free than under the German occupation." He understood that, during the Vichy period in France, each gesture had the weight of a commitment; teaching philosophy under fascism could become an act of heroic citizenship. In relation to Iran, I often say, "We have never been more free than under the Islamic Republic." It sounds paradoxical, as the Revolution sounded the death knell for critical intellectualism, but in recent years, a new generation has given critical intellectualism a new, vibrant life. In a country like Iran, where the logic of the theological-political is still absolute and where there is a single way of organizing the society, the principal goal of critical intellectuals is to fight for a pluralism of ethical values and for different modes of social co-existence. This is to say, the chief task of Iranian intellectualism is to establish the proper balance between philosophical questioning and political decency.

The suffocation of intellectualism by the unreasonable and violent radicalism of the early years of the Iranian Revolution (on both the left and the right) seriously injured our common sense ways of political thought and political action and led to deep confusion about questions of moral responsibility and collective human solidarity. But the new thinking rejects any existing consensus, whether in a traditional authority or a modern ideology, because it calls for the institutionalization of the public debate in the form of rational argument. The real dividing line between the younger generation of Iranian intellectuals and the previous generations, especially those on the left, is between the admirers of dialogue and a plurality of values on one hand and the preachers of grand narratives and utopian ideas on the other. The point is that Iranian intellectuals are no longer entitled to play the role of prophet or hero. Their public role is to demystify ideological fanaticisms, not to preach them. Today, the sentimental, leftist view of the intelligentsia as the vanguard of an ideology is inadequate.

What all this means is that Iranian intellectualism has finally returned to earth, to the here and now, after decades of looking for salvation in ultimate solutions. Perhaps this is why philosophy is now so fashionable among younger Iranians. Because it is, we need to recognize that the struggle for the empowerment of critical thinking in Iran is a day-to-day challenge that is not only intellectual but social and cultural. Philosophy is not a classroom where you sit passively and listen to others for the rest of your life. It is about responsible civic participation and intellectual integrity. Pascal was right when he said, "We are usually convinced more easily by reasons we have found ourselves than by those which have occurred to others." This is very true of our situation in Iran. The critical actors in Iranian society need to find their own logics and ways of working together rather than adopting those imposed on them. But this cannot be done without intellectual maturity. Maturity is the necessary precondition for pluralism to be able to take root in Iranian society. Thinking about democracy and establishing democratic governance in a country like Iran is not an easy task. Despite what some people think, it is more than a simple political enterprise. We have grown accustomed to living with political evil and not thinking about it. We live with a culture of violence while remaining unaware of the ways we have reproduced it in our everyday lives. (I am always surprised by the number of people in Iranian cities who take their children to watch the hanging of a man or woman in the public space.) The challenge here is more philosophical. Our modes of thinking and judging are crucial in determining where Iran can go from here. The process of democratic consciousness-building can provide continuity for the political structures of democracy. This is where philosophical thinking comes to our aid as a grammar of resistance to the tyranny of our authoritarian traditions. This does not mean that the tremendous body of traditions in Iran are mere errors of the past. We find ourselves at home in our traditions, after all. But we need to distinguish between a false sense of belonging and a respect for a common space where the plurality of voices can be heard.

I am in full sympathy with a mode of thinking that would bring intellectuals into the struggle against thoughtlessness and acceptance of things as they are and against appealing to authority, to tradition, or to personal loyalty. Here, I believe, lies the deep paradox between living in and for truth and the commitment to a culture where one feels at home. Today, an independent and critical thinker who takes responsibility for the marginal status thrust upon him or her is like an acrobat walking on a tightrope.

When I look back at myself sitting on a chair in the interrogation room, blindfolded and facing the wall, I see just such an acrobat tumbling from the tightrope, all the while wondering whether a victim of political evil can react rationally, particularly while locked in solitary confinement. What kind of a psychological defence mechanism could help me cope with the devastating situation I found myself in? Were my emotional trauma and responses comparable to those of individuals who, like my father, face terminal cancer? Upon learning of his terminal illness, my father said just two words: "Why me?" And in prison, I asked the same question. Political prisoners have good reason to feel angry—after all, their lives have been interrupted and they no longer have control of their future. But although there is no certainty about tomorrow, there is always hope.

Hafiz of Shiraz says, "I wish I could show you when you are lonely or in darkness the astonishing light of your own being." Since hope never passes into certainty or has any bearing on the future, it is built upon patience. For we Iranians, hopefulness is not a way of simply seeing or acting but of being. Our capacity to hope has been shaped by our historical destiny, which, depending on its differing moments and experiences, has provided us space to hope and for hope. We all have a beautiful way to hope and to adapt. When I thought about hope, I saw beyond my solitary confinement and the interrogation rooms to the mystical power of the human mind. I thought of what Primo Levi calls "man's capacity to dig himself in, to secrete a shell, to build around himself a tenuous barrier of defence." I lived in solitude, which was painful, but hope is delicious as a horizon to gaze on in order to attain maturity. Those who are incapable of hope live in vain; they can never be happy, fulfilled, or satisfied. They do not live. As Seneca would say, they are getting ready to live. As such, solitude became my sole companion in my solitary confinement. Memories became my true friends. I lived with them and I listened to them. Truly, seeking out memories takes away the pain of everyday life, especially when one is in prison.

5

TWO DAYS AFTER MY ARREST, AT 10:00 A.M. I WAS handcuffed, blindfolded, and led to a car where two heavy-weight security officers awaited me. Another car bearing three more men followed us. I was astonished when the car drew up outside my apartment building. They gave me my keys and asked me to open the door of my apartment and to make sure that my wife would not make any noise. As it happened, my mother and my in-laws were there, too, all of them very worried about what had happened to me. They were happy to see that I was alive and in good health, although they could tell from my tired, unshaven face that I had had two rough nights at the prison.

As soon as the security officers came in, they began searching for documents or papers that might give cre-dence to their conspiracy theory. One of them filmed the whole scene and looked in the cupboards for pirated DVDs and alcohol. My mother tried her best to reason with my jailers, hoping to persuade them to have mercy. I was told to sit on a chair and remain silent. I could not say a word about my situation in prison. The security officers confiscated most of my writings and photos, finishing their four-hour search by taking five big boxes of documents back to the prison.

I will never forget what my mother told me before they led me away. "My son," she said, "stand firm for your convictions. Your father also went to prison." These words gave me confidence and courage. The jailers put the handcuffs back on me, blindfolded me again, and took me back to Section 209. My mother's words rang in my ears, and they reminded me of Rumi's: "Ignore those who make you fearful and sad, who degrade you back towards disease and death."

IN THE DAYS that followed—full of lonely hours when I had nothing to keep me company except my thoughts—I fought to hold on to my beliefs. Solitary confinement made me lose my faith in faith, but it taught me to believe in conscience. Solitary confinement can easily strip away human dignity, but some prisoners find the means to refuse to give up their dignity and are able to move toward a greater humanity. My jailers tried hard to convince me that life itself isn't worth much because they were in a position to destroy it. I had always believed that the fact of life itself surmounts despair. Being in solitary helped me understand this much better. I learned that the true meaning of life is always discovered at times when its very essence is in question.

There is nothing comparable to solitary confinement in a country like Iran. Its high-security prisons were built for only one purpose: to dehumanize, torture, punish, and destroy those men and women who dare to think independently. Evin Prison signifies not only the failure of three thousand years of Persian civilization but also the defeat of all common sense. In Section 209, the interrogations, tortures, and other degrading punishments are motivated by pure sadism. Until I grasped this, I had a hard time understanding why my interrogators enjoyed humiliating me so much, as if it gave them prestige. They constantly attempted to shake my ideas, to chip away at their foundations, to make me feel guilty about the political decisions I had made. Their purpose was to make me believe that I had betrayed my country; their method was sadism.

I resolved to keep my mind lucid and to make my reason work to counter this lunacy and the surrealistic situation in which I was living. The light in my cell was on twenty-four hours a day, making it difficult for me to keep track of time. But I soon realized that I could track the morning, noon, and evening *azan* (call to prayer). I could barely sleep, no more than three hours each night, as the feeling of being watched every hour woke me up. I was taken off for further interrogation at any time of the day or night. I spent up to eight hours a day in the interrogation room, my only contact with other humans. It is deeply ironic that the only time a prisoner of conscience is out of solitary confinement is during interrogations.

During the first fifty days of my imprisonment I was not permitted to go up to the rooftop terrace, but later I was allowed to spend fifteen minutes every week there. I could take off my blindfold and look at the sky through the bars that covered the rooftop. I felt like a canary in a cage—although I was never in the mood to sing like a canary. The terrace was quite large—some thirty metres square—so I could jog around it. I never met any other prisoner there. Only a prisoner who has been confined for long behind high walls can appreciate the psychological value of these outings. I loved these outside walks, and the view of the Iranian sky added a joy that went a long way to removing the bitterness of solitary confinement. I filled my mind with the beautiful floating clouds and took them back to my cell. I was almost jealous of the clouds. They reminded me of a poem by Yeats: "I know that I shall meet my fate somewhere among the clouds above; those

that I fight I do not hate, those that I guard I do not love."
I had never noticed nature the way I did during my time
in solitary. Prevented from indulging in normal routines
of life, I became more observant of nature's ways around
me. I started watching the insects that came to my cell.
I realized that while I was complaining of loneliness, I
had life in my proximity. All these crawling animals went
on with their usual patterns of living without paying any
attention to me. I used to watch the ants busy at work in
a corner of my cell. They seemed to be very happy, and
I think it is because they were so busy preparing for the
winter. While I watched them, I was ashamed of myself
for being idle. Then there were cockroaches who visited
me at night. Every night I could hear one or two of them
crawling into my cell through the tiny gap between the
iron door and the concrete floor. They seemed to pass
within an inch of my feet, and I was always afraid of walking on them. These unwelcomed visits broke the monotony
and dullness of prison life. I preferred their company to
that of my interrogators.

I used to get up very early in the morning. Partly this
was due to going to bed early and partly because of the
Morning Prayer call played on the prison loudspeakers.
For breakfast we had tea and cheese, and in the evening
we usually had a piece of chicken sausage with rice or
pickles and thin bread that tasted of paper. For lunch, we

usually had rice mixed with lentils or served with a stew, the main ingredients of which were cheap meat, tomatoes, lentils, onion, and lemon. My interrogations started in the morning and usually ended after lunchtime, so I usually found my food resting cold on my prison plate. Every week one of the guards would ask for a small amount of money from what I had had with me when I was arrested and a list of things I needed. I don't smoke, so I usually asked for tissues and biscuits. I used the back of the boxes to write down aphorisms.

From the very first days of my imprisonment I had to fight moments of despair. I frequently had headaches and stomach aches, and I was once taken to the prison doctor, who gave me a few Aspirins. He looked very young and inexperienced. I supposed he had to keep silent about all the suffering that he saw. I found it strange that the doctors and interrogators could spend their days interrogating and torturing people and then return home at night to kiss their wives and children as if nothing had happened. In Iran, women are expected to submit to the will of their fathers and husbands; mothers are glorified but their lives are circumscribed by sharia law, and emancipated women are viewed as agents of degeneracy and religious decline. Wives are not supposed to ask about the fate of the prisoners their husbands interrogated or tortured during the day. The wives and mothers of torturers provide their husbands or sons with the semblance of normality at home. Some women do more than this: they are police officers and prison guards and most probably perpetrators of violence against other women.

I could sometimes hear the voices of female inmates from afar after I was moved to a different cell, where I spent the final seventy days of my imprisonment. This cell was the last one before a stairwell. Near this stairwell was a public phone where prisoners could speak with their families for a few short minutes in the presence of their guards. Every week I was upset by the cries of a woman on the phone to a child she missed terribly. It reminded me of my own daughter and how much I missed her. There is always suffering, and man is wolf to man: an old story. But suffering is not all there is. And we can fight against the dark even when we are powerless. Powerlessness appeared to me as moral innocence, but it made me feel complicit with the designs of my jailers. From the start of my incarceration, I refused to be tamed by the iron hand of solitary confinement. I went back to what I knew best, which was reading and writing. I remembered this saying by Jorge Luis Borges: "A writer—and I believe, generally all persons—must think that whatever happens to him or her is a resource. All things have been given to us for a purpose, and an artist must feel this more intensely. All that happens to us, including our humiliations, our

– 47 –

misfortunes, our embarrassments, all is given to us as raw material, as clay, so that we may shape our art."

I asked for something to read and was told that I was allowed only the *Qur'an* and a book of stories on early Islam. I have never been a religious man, although I have always had an inclination toward spiritual matters, so I said that was fine. They brought me an Arabic edition of the *Qur'an* that had a Persian translation, and I read it from beginning to end five times. This was not the first time I had read the *Qur'an*, but I had never spent this much time with a holy book. In it I discovered wisdom that went far beyond my captors' narrow interpretations. I tried to understand why the *Qur'an* is invoked among Muslims to support directly contradictory positions— some Muslims consider it a book of peace and others use it to legitimize mass murder. Of course, in all religions we can find extremists who use dogma as the only lens through which to view the tough realities of our world. But extremists do not necessarily offer us the best understanding of religious texts. Reading a holy book does not go hand in hand with extremism. Re-reading the *Qur'an* did not make a dogmatic man out of me although, as a philosopher, I was willing to approach the text without prejudice and without fear.

The book of stories about Islam was the same thick book that my grandmother used to read every day after

Check Out Receipt

Banks Public Library
503-324-1382
http://www.wccls.org/libraries/banks

Monday, October 1, 2018 2:41:45 PM

Item: 190384468
Title: BAL ILL TIME WILL SAY NOTHING
Material: Inter-Library Loans
Due: 10/15/2018

Total items: 1

Thanks for visiting the Banks Library!

prayer. When I was a kid, I was curious about it, but my grandmother never explained it to me. When I tried to read it, I couldn't understand one word. Now, after thirty years of philosophical practice, once again I found it incomprehensible. I skipped the paragraphs in Arabic and read the short stories in Persian, but they were also of no interest. A mediocre book has nothing to offer its readers no matter how closely we read it. Nevertheless these books were precious commodities in my hours of despair and solitude. Reading and writing were my paths to the truth inside the lie I was living. For me, the road to freedom is paved with words. I wanted to touch the art of living at every level of life. Reading and writing are modes of thinking, and a prisoner cannot survive except through his thoughts. His mind is his only weapon against tyranny. We lose everything when we lose our pride in thinking.

A few days after I was imprisoned, my interrogators ordered me to write an essay on everything that I knew about democratic uprisings in Eastern Europe, in line with their idea of the velvet revolution I was supposed to be fomenting in Iran. They wanted to use the essay to force a confession from me. They were convinced that deep down I was a revolutionary and intended to use radical ideas to undermine the stability of the nation. They were determined to prove that I was using social networks among intellectuals and artists in Iran to upset the status quo. In their view, my effort to establish cultural and intellectual links with the outside world was an unacceptable threat to the Iranian state. I was being forced to incriminate myself as a conspirator, as if history had thrown me up after a hangover. The most shocking fact about history is that the individual human beings that are its victims are condemned by the monstrous flux of history to suffer in conflicts not their own. Therefore, we live in history without history living for us. My historical perspective as a victim of history began the day I went to prison. Confession was not a way to accept my failings, because I knew that it would be history, not the confession, that would give me absolution. Ironically, I was asked to write about events without thinking about history.

At first, I told them that it would be too difficult for me to write such an essay without access to books and other materials. They insisted that I needn't worry and that everything I required would be provided. So I tried to do it in my own way. In writing this essay, I thought back to my experiences with politics from childhood on. Hajj Ali knew that my father had been a communist, but his claim that my father had failed and made wrong choices upset me deeply and showed me how much misunderstanding about history there is under the Islamic

Republic. My father, Amir-Hosein Jahanbegloo, under-took his intellectual journey in a very hostile political climate. In the 1950s, when he was in his late twenties, he joined the communist Tudeh Party, which had been banned after the 1953 coup d'état that deposed Prime Minister Mossadegh. He opposed the Shah's regime and was jailed briefly for his anti-government activities. But he was neither reckless nor dogmatic. He had an intellectual approach to politics, emphasizing compassion and, above all, education and development.

At home, he was a private man who slept apart from his family. He cherished his large library of books on philosophy, economy, literature, and sciences, which were shelved in dusty bookcases made of rich oak and seemed to me to hold the charm of history. Despite his private nature, he could be very sociable and had many friends, though he preferred serious, intimate relationships. He was stern and intimidating, but he was also handsome and well-liked. He was humble and full of empathy for others, but had a vigorous temper that erupted whenever his enthusiasm got the better of his judgement. He was loved by his family and respected by his friends and stu-dents. He loved his students, and he loved teaching, but he got to enjoy it only during the second stage of his life.

Shortly after my birth, my father started work as an economic consultant for the newly nationalized National

Iranian Oil Company. He was part of the Iranian delegation to OPEC meetings, and because of this would occasionally travel abroad. Each time he left, I was eager for him to come back home with toys and books for me. When my father was at home, I usually watched him from a distance; whenever I approached him it was with both timidity and admiration. In his room, he had a rocking chair where I would sometimes sit with him and read novels and detective stories as well as books on history and philosophy. He understood French and English and was deeply familiar with both the Western canon and Islamic mystical literature. One of his favourite authors was the medieval writer Azizuddin Nasafi and his book *İnsan-ı Kâmil* (The Book of the Perfect Human Being). He bought more than twenty copies of this book and offered them as gifts to his friends and students. He also admired Socrates and, like him, believed that true knowledge is knowing one's ignorance. He believed passionately in ideas and in the role that ideas play in our lives. For him, the true heroes of history were ideas, not people. It was not through writing but through teaching, which constituted his life's main work, that he tried to communicate the important ideas he had learned in life.

When I was four, my father threw me into the Caspian Sea. It is one of my earliest memories, and the act came to symbolize my relationship with my father. He threw me into life—into philosophy, into politics, and into history—in the same way. Just as I soon learned to swim in the rough waters of the Caspian, so I learned to navigate my way through the labyrinths of my early education. My father had studied economics at the Sorbonne in Paris as a student of Francois Perroux, the famous French economist and, having had the benefit of a liberal education and exposure to Western culture, he wanted me to have the same advantages, and more.

In those early years, my father would take me to the cinema on Thursday afternoons and afterward, from time to time, for ice cream and cream cakes at the Khoshmaram shop in downtown Tehran. I still remember the Persian-style ice cream my father and I shared. It had a creamy, custardy texture and the wonderful flavours of saffron, pistachios, and rosewater. My favourite movies were historical films, among them *Lawrence of Arabia*, *The Great Escape*, and *The Guns of Navarone*. *Lawrence of Arabia* is one of the greatest movie-going experiences I have ever had or ever will have. I saw the film three times as a kid and have seen it eighteen times since. It holds a very special place in my memory and is one of the films that inspired me to study history. I especially liked the dialogue between Prince Feisal and T.E. Lawrence, which goes like this:

PRINCE FEISAL: But you know, Lieutenant, in the Arab city of Cordoba were two miles of public lighting in the streets when London was a village?

T.E. LAWRENCE: Yes, you were great.

PRINCE FEISAL: Nine centuries ago.

T.E. LAWRENCE: Time to be great again, my lord.

From the very beginning of my education, I studied a wide variety of liberal arts subjects. Different settings and climates also shaped my cosmopolitan attitude toward the world. The boarding schools I was sent to in Shropshire, England, and Lausanne, Switzerland, provided me with formative and strange, yet interesting, experiences. My stay in Lausanne was short and painful. I was barely six and I hated to be separated from my parents, who lived at that time in Geneva, so I cried every night until my parents decided to take me back and send me to a primary school in Geneva. My Swiss experience left me with few other memories. My English experience, however, was much more adventurous. When I finished the sixth grade, my parents decided to make an English gentleman out of me. They consulted one of their friends, who had studied in England, and he suggested they enroll me at

Gordonstoun, which Prince Charles had attended on the recommendation of his father, the Duke of Edinburgh. I found out later that Prince Charles did not enjoy his stay at this school, which he characterized as "Colditz in kilts." Eventually, in the summer of 1968, my mother decided to accompany me to England and to register my name at another school—Nash Court, close to the city of Ludlow in Shropshire. Nash Court had been converted into a residential school by a local headmaster, Henry Lucas Oakley, in 1846. It was later taken over by the National Association of Boys' Clubs in 1948 and turned into a training base and camp site. It was a tough boys' school where we did a great deal of sports. The formal school uniform was a navy blazer with grey flannel pants, white shirt, and school tie. We had porridge for breakfast and shepherd's pie and English pudding for dinner. I have not touched any of these since my short time there. The shortcomings of English food aside, I admired English football teams and was very excited to go to the games once a week. I was proud of my ability to play on a team and to be able to learn a skillful and imaginative football. We had extensive training programs and some of us eventually had to decide whether we should stick with football or carry on with our education. For me, the decision was easy, since I never wanted to be a professional sportsman. I continued to practice soccer, basketball, and swimming until I graduated from high school, but I had no particular interest in the world of sports.

Life in Nash Court had strange, but funny, aspects. Curiously enough, it taught me that Englishmen were obsessed by ghosts. The school used to take us to visit English castles, including Ludlow Castle, which was said to be haunted by the ghost of sad Marion de la Bruyere, who had been re-enacting her dive to death from the Pendover Tower since the latter part of the twelfth century. The Hanging Tower of Ludlow Castle was said to contain the sounds of heavy breathing. My English companions were terrified by these ghost stories and, since I do not believe in ghosts, they challenged me to sleep alone in the large courtyard of our school, which was close to an old cemetery. In Iranian folklore, we do not have ghosts like those in European cultures, but there is the phenomenon of "jinn," which are supposed to be ugly and evil demons who have supernatural powers. These spiritual creatures inhabit an unseen world in a dimension beyond the visible universe, and Muslims believe that the only protection against them is to recite verses from the *Qur'an*. In any case, my lack of faith in jinns gave me courage to make a bet with my fellow campmates and to sleep without fear of any English ghost. One can add ghost haunting as an imaginative exercise to a plethora of inventive activities practiced at English boarding schools.

Despite these numerous assets, my parents saw that I returned to Tehran after a period of six months. After a year in a college preparatory high school in the heart of Tehran, I accompanied my parents to Algeria. My father had been sent on a mission to Algeria as the economic advisor for the newly born National Algerian Oil Company (SONATRACH) and we joined him few months later.

In contrast to my stay in England, my life with my family in post-independent Algeria between 1969 and 1970 was full of significant revelations. There, my parents were in close touch with many radicals, university students, and activists who had waged a continuous fight against colonialism and oppression. Algeria was still a revolutionary state, deeply socialist and connected with the Soviet Union, yet there was also an American presence. I remember vividly the day I came home from high school to our apartment to find three tall African American men standing in our living room with my mother. I gave her a questioning glance, but she merely gestured for me to go to my room and not interfere. Only later did I learn that these men were Black Panthers, in exile in Algeria, and that Eldridge Cleaver, one of their leaders, was among them. Such incidents were not unusual, although my parents did not let me get too involved in their affairs. They kept me at a distance to protect me from what they believed was dangerous ground for a young man. I clearly remember what happened after I wrote a ninth-grade essay on the Shah's White Revolution in which I criticized his Land Reforms Program. When I told my parents about my essay, they asked me to go to my teacher and tell him that I needed to revise my text in order to get a better grade. My teacher, who was an intelligent man, had read my essay and suggested I write on another subject altogether.

Thanks to the liberal thinking of my mother and father, my childhood and teenage years were not regulated by religious laws and my creativity was not subjected to the accusatory finger of Iranian and Islamic traditions. I was protected by my parents from the dangers of political evil. Later, I refused to continue being a detached spectator of society and history and got involved in politics. This meant I had to abandon my cherished security. Since then I have had my own share of suffering and sorrow, but they have taken nothing away from the wonderful experiences that were given to me by my parents.

My mother gave birth to me when she was only twenty-three. She had spent some time in the United Kingdom studying playwriting at the Old Vic theatre in London. She later went to Paris and decided to become an actress, but was dissuaded by some artist friends who suggested that she return to Iran. A strong and stubborn woman, she was already a radical-minded person, although with

no political affiliations, when she met my father; her radicalism, however, always started from an artistic point
of view. She was not an atheist and always had strong
spiritual aspirations. In the 1960s and the early 1970s
she wrote and directed many plays that were avant-garde
and sometimes political; some of the actors playing her
characters were even arrested for being radicals. When I
was only eight or nine, I used to go to rehearsals of her
plays. It was fun sitting all by myself in a grand theatre,
watching the actors. Her love for art extended to all its
different forms and had a huge influence on my life.

Amid these recollections, a flash from my teenage
years transports me to another place. Some of the actors
my parents were friendly with would come to our house
in Tehran every week. Among them was a young and
voluptuous woman, whom I idealized. She was more alive
in my fantasies than in reality, and the attraction I felt
for her was heightened by my fear of her mysterious,
female otherness. My boyish need for feminine nurture
and approval was accompanied by the romantic fantasy
of male sexual power and dominance that I had learned
from Hollywood actors like Humphrey Bogart and James
Cagney. She had beautiful juicy lips, which she coloured
with a shade of red that flattered her complexion. Each
time she came to our house, whatever taboos I had learned
from traditional Persian culture melted like snowflakes

on a windowpane and my sole desire was to kiss her in the way I had seen my heroes kiss women in the movies.

One day when she came for a visit to our house I took her to my room and started working my fingers through her hair and brushing my lips against her cheeks. I still remember the scent of her warm breath and the smell of her perfume. And then I found her lips and kissed her in the Hollywood way I was dying to imitate. I know now that it is through innocent adolescent experiences like that first carnal kiss that a basic instinct of being alive is awakened and we begin to understand ourselves.

When I was six and we were living in Geneva, my mother took me to Italy. I have vague memories of the museums we visited in Rome and Florence and various paintings of Saint Sebastian by Italian Renaissance painters. Later, when I was eleven, she took me to France so that I could see Beckett's and Ionesco's plays and gaze at the wonders of the Louvre. She also wanted me to learn to watch life closely, with sharp eyes, not that I understood that at the time. Thinking back on it now, it is no wonder that I turned out the way I did. For me, passion—even political passion—has always been induced through art and a multi-perspective view of life.

Even in Tehran, where I spent most of my childhood, I was exposed to many different aspects of society; there was a permeable line between the upper-middle-class intellectual and artistic atmosphere at home and the ordinary life of mid-twentieth-century Iran that lay beyond it. All kinds of intellectuals and artists regularly gathered at our large house in northern Tehran. Poets like Forough Farrokhzad, Sohrab Sepehri, Nader Naderpour, and Bijan Jalali, usually introverted, revealed their intimate sides within those walls. Naderpour had an obsessive habit of washing his hands. He always arrived very late for dinner and stayed very late. My father and I would go to bed, leaving him to talk about poetry and art with my mother. Sepehri was agoraphobic and felt uncomfortable in crowds. I remember him as a kind man with beautiful hands, more spiritual than religious, who became aggressive after too much wine. Farrokhzad was a sensitive woman and fine poet. One image of her has stayed in my mind: a disgusting scene at a party where I'd accompanied my parents. At one point, when many of the guests were drunk, Fourough was deliberately pushed into the swimming pool by some men. I suppose they were trying to humiliate her in front of the others because she was a talented poet and courageous. My father, who disliked male chauvinism, helped her out of the pool and took her back home. This incident is a powerful reminder of the sexism in Iranian intellectual life. Unfortunately, not much has changed since then, and the noisy chorus of male chauvinism continues to drown out the voices of reason. The dearest recollection I have of Sepehri is from a trip I went on with him, Bijan Jalali (who was the nephew of Sadegh Hedayat, the great Iranian writer), and my parents to the Caspian Sea when I was less than ten years old. At one point, I picked up a flat stone from the seashore and asked Sepehri and Jalali and most probably also my parents to sign it. Bijan Jalali kept the stone until his death in January 2000 and it is now in the possession of one of his friends.

One of the men I met in those years was the radical thinker Jalal Al-e-Ahmad, who was a very friendly and likable person. I criticized his extremist approach to politics in later years, but I will always remember his kindness toward me when I was a child. I still remember the time he bought me a soccer ball after I won a bet with him. This gentle man with greyish hair and a moustache rang our doorbell and asked for me to open the door. I went to the door and he handed me the soccer ball, saying, "*Ammou jan*, this is what I promised you." My father and Al-e-Ahmad were close friends and they joined the Tudeh Party practically at the same time, but Al-e-Ahmad later became a follower of Khalil Maleki, the anti-communist leader of the Toilers Party. My father started monthly meetings at our house to discuss philosophy, which came to be known as "Fardidieh," after Ahmad Fardid, a prominent Iranian philosopher who had studied in Germany and was a follower of Martin Heidegger. Al-Ahmad was among those who attended those meetings at our house. It was Fardid who coined the word "Westoxication," which was then popularized by Al-e-Ahmad in his widely known book *Gharbzadegi*. The Fardidieh meetings went on for more than fifteen years, and in the early 1970s philosophers such as Reza Davari Ardakani and Dariush Shayegan and literary critics such as Shahrokh Meskoob and Daryush Ashoori frequently attended them. My father was neither a follower of Fardid nor an admirer of Heidegger's thought, but he was deeply interested in philosophical debates. He always asked me to be present at these meetings but I had a hard time understanding the debates, which were usually about Iranian mystics and Western existential philosophy. Still, I gradually became familiar with the names Sartre, Heidegger, Jaspers, and Gabriel Marcel. I got my taste for philosophical inquiry from these monthly meetings at our house, as well as from the first philosophy books I read.

When I was thirteen I read Plato's *Republic* in Persian translation. After that I became interested in Socrates and read Karl Jasper's book *Socrates, Buddha, Confucius, Jesus*, a short excerpt from his larger work *Great Philosophers*. My interest in philosophy deepened through these readings and under the guidance of my father, who never pushed me to be an engineer or an economist like himself. I owe my lifelong love affair with books and reading to him. I had free run of his library as long as I asked his permission first and was careful with the covers of the books I read. For several years, my favourite novelists were the great storytellers Ernest Hemingway, John Steinbeck, Jules Verne, Alexandre Dumas, Victor Hugo, Jack London, and Honoré de Balzac. Then suddenly at the age of thirteen, my curiosity about philosophy made me turn to Dostoevsky, Tolstoy, and Kazantzakis. *The Idiot* by Dostoevsky was my father's favourite novel. I think he was fascinated by Prince Myshkin's moral reasoning when, at a crucial moment in the novel, just before Rogozhin tries to stab him, he argues with himself that the single law of humanity must be compassion.

I found that same compassion in Kazantzakis's character Zorba the Greek, who teaches a writer who has reached an impasse to live optimistically and instinctively. Like my father, I have always loved Zorba, who in a Nietzschean sense calls us to live life in a Dionysian way. Zorba is a passionate human being. He does everything intensely and fervidly, whether he is dancing, working in a mine, or embracing a woman. He expresses his emotions fully: he is not afraid to weep or laugh, to love or hate. My father admired Zorba's impulsive excesses, which showed him how to "cut the string in two" and be free. He wanted to be such a person, even as history turned him into a pessimist. We used to dance together to the theme song by the Greek composer Mikis Theodorakis for the film *Zorba the Greek*.

Aside from these busy, smoky gatherings, our house witnessed both hours of quiet contemplation and thunder from our record players. My father loved music and whenever I wandered from room to room I would be accompanied by Vivaldi's *Four Seasons*, Mozart's *Requiem*, or Edith Piaf's "Non, je ne regrette rien." From his radical past, he retained a love for his Russian records—large, heavy discs that blasted nationalistic songs like "Kalinka" and "The Cossacks." These songs have lingered long in my mind, and now it's impossible for me to disassociate them from my memories of our old home.

Beyond its walls lay another world, which I wandered into as often as I could. When I was young I was rarely allowed to leave the house alone. Our garden was large enough for me to play games with friends—the ones who joined me in pretending to be Tom Sawyer and Huck Finn—but by the time I reached my early teenage years, I wanted to venture farther. In nearby streets, I made new friends and fell in love with soccer. We used to play everywhere: on concrete courtyards, grassy fields, and dirt pitches, under sun or rain. And while we played, nothing else mattered. No barriers divided us, no political differences mattered, no social divisions constrained us. In those years, Tehran was still a clean and under-populated city where people lived safely and with dignity. Prior to the Revolution of 1979, the huge gardens and old houses of Tehran had not yet been replaced with fashionable high-rises and ugly buildings. The atmosphere was not polluted and we could see Mount Damavand and the blue sky.

The neighbourhood where we lived in the 1960s and 1970s was like a village, with a mix of traditionalist and modernist social classes living together. I could hear the call to prayer from three different mosques. Some of our neighbours, like Farrokh Ghaffari, who was one of the vice-presidents of National Iranian Television and a talented film director during the Shah's time, were from rich, aristocratic families, while others had gardens that were guarded and managed by working-class families whose children I used to play with on the dirt road in front of our house. We spent our summer days playing soccer, running around, swimming, and climbing trees. Ghaffary had two beautiful afghan hounds that, particularly in comparison with my Cairn terrier, were very elegant and graceful. I also had a black dog that, in contrast to her fur, had a soul as pure and white as snow. I remember the day when my father decided to take her to our orange garden in Shahsavar, near the Caspian Sea. The poor animal looked sad, as if she was being taken away to the slaughterhouse. Surprisingly, two months later she came back. To this day, I have not yet found an answer to the question: how did my dog travel 257 kilometres to get back home to Tehran?

I usually started my summers studying math, science, and philosophy with my father. He would take me to an English bookshop and buy me books on math games and beginners' geometry. I have never been very strong in math and physics as I don't have a mathematical mindset, but I liked biology and especially zoology. I spent a great deal of time watching the behaviour of various animals. I would catch insects and keep them in a bottle. We had all sorts of venomous creatures such as tarantulas and big wasps in our garden, and once our gardener caught a snake swimming in our pool. Early spring was the best time of the year, when the baby animals were born. One of my most exciting childhood experiences was watching the birth of a lamb. It was a thrilling experience to discover a newborn creature, full of excitement and a mystery that usually remained unexplained by the adults. Our gardener would always let me know a few hours before the event. It is a great experience for a child to see an animal being born. Still, I am certain that dipping children into the bloody realities of nature does not make them invulnerable to the harshness of life. Animals kill, but they don't imprison, torture, or build concentration camps.

As I went on reliving my memories of those remote childhood experiences, lost in reverie when I was supposed to be writing an essay on revolutions, the harsh bell of reality kept ringing in my ears, pulling me out of the dream and bringing me face to face with the ugly side of life. I suddenly saw the figure of the little boy that I used to be turn into a man of fifty sitting in his jail cell. None of this sweetness of childhood would last, I realized; it would all disappear, crumbling under the weight of ideology and ignorance. One final memory cast its bitterness over everything and made it clear to me why I was sitting in a gloomy cell. It was from March 1979, nearly a decade after I had left those childhood games behind and gone to France to study philosophy. I had just returned to Tehran, where the Islamic Revolution was in full swing and the Islamic revolutionaries had consolidated their power over the nation. I got in touch with one of my childhood friends, Davood, the son of our gardener, and discovered that he was now a fervent supporter of the Revolution. He and some other young men had occupied a house that belonged to one of the Shah's cousins and they invited me to go with them to have a look around the place to see the decadence and celebrate its fall. Davood showed me around the house and pointed out a large collection of books.

"You should have these, Ramin. You've always been an intellectual, so I'm sure you'd find them useful in your studies. Anyhow, you would find them more useful than we would," he said, chuckling and nodding to his comrades.

I thought about it for a while, but in the end my conscience wouldn't let me steal them.

I said, "It's not right for me to take them. I think we should give them away somewhere else. I have some other books that I no longer have any use for, so maybe we could combine them with these and give them to the local mosque, so that they can build a small library that others can use."

They liked this idea, and we went through with the plan. By the time the little library was established in my neighbourhood mosque I was delighted. In fact, I was so excited that I came up with the absurd idea of giving a lecture to inaugurate the opening of the library. The first person I went to with this thought in mind was my father.

"You want to do what? What are you talking about? What kind of lecture do you intend to give?"

"I want to talk about Marcuse, about reason and revolution. I think they would understand, what with everything that's happening these days."

My father merely shrugged, but I knew his reaction was a bad omen. Still, I went ahead, stubborn and anxious to share the philosophical concepts I had just discovered.

It was, of course, a fiasco. At the mosque, in front of a small group of religious radicals, I delivered a long-winded speech about the Frankfurt School and its contributions to modern political thinking, about the nature of the dialectic, about instrumental rationality, radical subjectivity, and alienation. As I droned on about revolutionary potential, emancipation, and authenticity they stared at me, bewildered. I might as well have been speaking gibberish. They asked no questions and dispersed without bothering to speak to me after I had finished. I was staggered—crushed. How could I not have known that the days of mutual understanding were over? How could I have failed to notice that the innocent games we played as teenagers had turned into political games in which lives were on the line, ignorance prevailed, and immeasurable distances separated the space of our childhood from a mob of dogmatic revolutionaries? History and politics have never been kind to Iranians, perhaps because they never took them seriously. Or perhaps because there was one notable deficiency in Iranian history: common sense. I was deep in these thoughts when a guard opened my cell door and announced that I had a visitor.

6

FIFTY DAYS HAD PASSED SINCE MY ARREST AND, although I had been keeping track by making scratches on the wall, it was hard to believe it had been that long. In ordinary life, fifty days often carry little weight. They flit by as we go about our daily tasks, caught in the flow of modern life. When one is alone in prison, sleepless, and under constant pressure, days become heavy and oppressive. Each hour is another stone on one's back. It is a different kind of suffering from physical torture: it spares the body and goes directly for the soul. And yet, despite the difficulties I was facing, I was always aware that others had gone through worse ordeals.

Few people know suffering the way Iranian women do. Those who had lived through the Revolution, who had lived *with* the Revolution, had suffering tattooed on their souls. It was a disease they passed on to their sons and daughters, and one they bore with courage and anger. The Iranian ultra-conservative faction has always reserved a special kind of hostility for women, suppressing them in as many ways as it can. This is because it fears them most. It recognizes their spirit, their outrage, their willingness to fight, and it responds with rancour and abuse. In thinking about how to cope with my suffering, I continually looked to Iranian women for examples. On that very day, a sweltering day in June, thousands of them were protesting yet again in the streets of Tehran, bringing many of them the misfortune of landing where I was.

It was also on that fiftieth day that Azin came. She came to bring me a hint of salvation.

All the time I had been sitting in my cell, fighting to keep my sanity, not knowing how my wife and child were doing, she had been fighting to see me and to get me out. The day after my arrest, the participants in the European conference I was supposed to attend in Brussels had become concerned, and one of them, Ron Asmus, whom I had met in 2002 at a conference in Istanbul, had contacted Azin to tell her I had not arrived. My wife and my mother had been left without any news of me for forty-eight hours, until I was taken home by guards for the search of my home.

It did not take Azin and my mother long to take up the Herculean task of contacting everyone they could and pulling every string they had to get me released. Azin met secretly with the Italian ambassador, my friend Roberto Toscano, throwing on a chador and going through the back door of his residence in the Farmanieh neighbourhood of Tehran to tell him what had happened to me. She, Roberto, and his wife, Francesca, had talked about me and cried together. Roberto was ready to do anything he could to help me. I have rarely met another diplomat like him. The French president Charles de Gaulle used to say, "Diplomats are useful only in fair weather. As soon as it rains they drown in every drop." But Roberto was not one to waste time. He knew how to swim in dangerous waters. As a diplomat in Chile, he had saved many lives during the coup d'état in 1973. Today, he is no longer a diplomat, but I am pretty sure that as a dear friend, who has co-authored two books with me, he would go to the same trouble to get me out of prison.

With Roberto's help, talks soon began with members of the Council of the European Union. Javier Solana, the Secretary General of the council, was contacted, and a petition was started, which was passed first throughout Europe and later through Canada, the United States, India, and many other places. I had no clue that any of this was happening. I knew I had friends and sympathizers out there, but I never imagined the scale of their response, the generosity and the compassion they showed during my time of crisis. Later, when Azin told me about the international support, I cried with surprise and appreciation. It was truly a testament to the consciousness and decency of intellectuals everywhere.

But I didn't learn any of this when Azin came with Afarin, our one-year-old daughter, in her arms and stood outside the gates in the unbearable heat until she could see me. Massive arrests had been made that day during the demonstration for women's rights and dozens of protestors had been brought straight to Evin. While they were being processed, visitors simply had to wait. When the guard came to my cell that afternoon and announced that I had a visitor, I was confused, and then, when my thoughts cleared up and I realized who my visitor must be, I became very excited.

Preparing me for the visit was a ridiculous process. Hajj Ali retrieved some of the clothes I had been planning to wear at the conference and told me to put them on. They shaved me so that I no longer looked like the Count of Monte Cristo, and Hajj Ali even insisted on spraying me with cologne. All this was meant to make me look presentable and in good shape. There was good reason for this, as I was to learn later, but at the time my captors told me nothing and, to be honest, as thrilled as I was, it barely mattered to me. I was blindfolded and escorted out of Section 209, then put into a car and driven past the inner gates, down from the secluded hilly area to the main gate where the visiting rooms and the guards' dormitories are.

We had just ten minutes together. Before I entered the room where Azin was waiting for me, Hajj Ali told me this and emphasized it. Ten minutes. And, he whispered, I was not to forget what he had told me: if I said anything about what had gone on in prison I would not be able to see Azin again. He sat me down on a sofa next to her and removed my blindfold. Seeing her took my breath away. She seemed very excited and, as her large, searching eyes looked me over, I could tell her heart was beating fast. Afarin was clinging to her tightly, obviously scared by the filthy, gloomy place. It was not a regular visiting room. The sofa we sat on was dirty and full of holes, and the walls were covered with stains and chipped paint. In the corner there were some pillows and blankets, which I assumed were for guards to sleep under. We were in this room so that other prisoners and visitors could not see me. I was nervous and didn't know what to say. We wanted to embrace, but Hajj Ali was sitting right there, behind a desk in front of us. So we sat on the sofa staring at each other.

She kept asking, "How are you doing? Is everything okay?" and I said, over and over, "Yes, I'm fine. Are you okay?"

There was so much else that I wanted to say, but the words kept fading as soon as they reached my lips.

"Don't bring Afarin here anymore. I don't want her to have any memories of this," I finally said.

Azin gave me a knowing look, then reached into her bag and took out three books: the autobiographies of Gandhi and Nehru and Hegel's *Phenomenology of Spirit*.

"These will help," she said. She knew exactly why.

Hajj Ali took the books away from me immediately and informed me that they would have to be checked. Most books were fine, he said, but any notations or sections not written by the author were forbidden: they could contain secret messages. Then he told us that our time was up.

The departure was hurried—there was barely any time for the pain to set in. As we kissed goodbye, Azin leaned over and whispered in my ear, "Everything is okay outside. Be strong." And I found strength in her words. Even as I was taken back to the bleakness of my cell, even as I changed back into my prison clothes, I was filled with new hope and determination. Soon, I told myself, I will leave this place, and I'll be together again with my wife and child.

But back in my cell, I began to be tormented by different thoughts. The memory of Azin's farewell kiss brought back reminders of my short married life. We were married in August 2004 and Afarin was born a year later. Nothing in my life has been better than having a daughter, nor will anything else ever measure up to it. My daughter is the greatest gift life has given me and my greatest joy. She has filled my life with love and hope. After all, a child's love is the only thing that cannot be bought or sold or earned. Love from children is instinctive, while from adults it is more meditated and non-spontaneous. Children know exactly where to stand between our hopes and our misfortunes. I hold this question as a guiding principle in my life: "What do I really need to be happy?" What I come to over and over again is that only the love and kindness of my daughter will really make me happy in any enduring way. If the meaning of life is to add value to it and to be happy, then each moment of a child's love is worth an age of dullness. Children wear their happiness and sadness without guilt. I certainly have been guilty of trying to be happy, but happiness dislikes those who consume it without producing it. So I turned to women to show me happiness, understanding that being happy is something I had to learn from them rather than taking from them.

All through my life, I have wanted not only to be loved by women but also to be understood by them. So long as I was loved by a woman I felt useful to myself. The force a man turns on himself to make himself loved is sometimes more cruel than not being loved in return.

The main reason my first marriage failed is that I wanted to love my wife wisely but not fully. This I deeply regret and I wish I could relive the past, which cannot happen. The saddest thing about life is that it only happens once.

I met my first wife, Mania, after my return to Iran in 1992. She was the daughter of Mahmoud Javadipour, an Iranian painter who was famous after the Second World War for his post-impressionist paintings. Strange destiny: Mania was an architect, like Azin, my second wife, and they were exactly the same age. Each stands for a different period in my life, representing a complementary or opposing ideal that inspired the evolution of my intellectual thought.

Yet while I had relationships with dozens of women, and was true to most of them—especially my first wife— each of these women shines out as a crucial catalyst in my development as a man. However, I always remember what Picasso told his mistress Françoise Gilot in 1943: "Women are machines for suffering." I was married to Mania in September 1993, shortly after we were introduced to each other at a music party in Tehran. I was back in the country after my father's death, and my mother was struggling with all sorts of wicked people who were trying to take away our beloved house. I should have stayed with my mother, but we had trouble getting along together in the absence of my father. Now I feel guilty about having gotten married, abandoning her and my grandmother. Was it selfishness? Was it ambition? I don't know, but my decision certainly changed many things in my life. My mother sacrificed a great part of her life to care for my grandmother, and maybe I should have done the same for her. It goes without saying that true love requires self-sacrifice. There is something spiritual about loving that many of us are unable to understand. Love is the deepest metaphysical dimension of humanity. It is the knowledge of the heart as thinking is the knowledge of the mind. Happiness is where our hearts and minds come together.

The most memorable encounter in this period of my life was with Bijan Jalali, the Iranian poet, whom I had not seen since the 1960s. I was among the rare visitors to his old family house in a beautiful area of Tehran. He was now in his mid-sixties and spent his life on the margin of Iranian society—not just physically, but also mentally. A man of ecstatic sensibility, Jalali had an anguished awareness of the world, a self-consciousness that invited self-examination and caused him to seek out otherness in Iranian society. Through his poetic dialogue with the world, Jalali wanted to feel its pulse and vitality while redefining humanity's destroyed soul. He loved animals more than humans and was always surrounded by cats and dogs. He was the Iranian expression of Saint Francis

of Assisi, who praised all the creations of God. In 1996
I decided to make a documentary on him. I borrowed a
video camera from one of my friends and spent a few days
conversing with Jalali about his poetry and life. Despite
our age difference we were very close, and he shared with
me many of his thoughts and poems, which I liked very
much. I always regretted the shortness of this vibrant
friendship, which was ended by his sudden death in January 2000 while I was in Canada.

There are many people to whom I owe something
in life. One of them was Shahrokh Meskoob, my parents' close friend, whom I called "Amu Shahrokh" (Uncle
Shahrokh). Meskoob was an outstanding writer, literary historian, and social critic and a prominent voice of
moral intellectualism. But what I liked most about him
was his humanism. He was a gentle and angelic man
who for decades regaled me with his humorous, folksy
tales and with innumerable acts of kindness. His social
and literary life was distinguished by his commitment to
ethical principles and the self-critical attitude that ideally
informs the life of a true intellectual. It was his humanistic values that led him first to immerse himself in Fer-
dowsi's *Book of Kings* and later to join the Tudeh Party,
which was outlawed in 1949. Not unlike Julien Benda,
the French philosopher and author of *The Treason of the
Intellectuals*, Meskoob, unlike most Iranian intellectuals of

his generation, firmly believed in universal human values. He believed Iran's future should be closely tied to social and political developments in democratic nations. It has always been impossible for me to think about Meskoob and not remember my father. They were very close, because neither was egocentric and both despised false pretensions. Amu Shahrokh became a kind of a mentor for me during my days in Paris in the 1980s and 1990s. He was the first person to read and comment on my writings, and I would share my political views with him. He was also the first person who gave me the sad news about my father's death in Iran and shared my grief and my tears. I still share his memory with Amu Hassan—Hassan Kamshad—another close friend of my family, who knew Meskoob closely and has new and interesting things to say about him. Shahrokh Meskoob was also one of my witnesses at my first marriage in 1993.

During our stay in Iran in the 1990s, Mania and I lived in a small studio on Gandhi Street in Tehran that I had exchanged for my apartment in Paris. I suffered from a stomach ailment and my problems with the Iranian system did not help it. From my first trip to Iran in October 1992 until I left in September 1997, I was under constant pressure from the authorities. The journal *Kayhan* attacked me as an anti-Islamic and anti-revolutionary intellectual. I could not find a job at the university and in 1993 I was fired from the Academy of Philosophy after six months. I started working with the Farzan Publishing House, which was financed by Dariush Shayegan, an old friend of my parents and a French-speaking philosopher with whom I did a book of conversations.

I have known Shayegan most of my life and hold him in esteem as a human being and as an intellectual. Civilized, imaginative, self-critical, Shayegan is a marvellously gifted observer of our world. He is a man of extreme refinement, sensibility, and great humanistic virtue, with a deep taste for metaphysics. He has always been a big help to me during difficult times in my life. I will never forget the day in 1974 that he took me to a tailor's shop in Tehran to buy me a suit for my high-school graduation ceremony. When I returned to the country after the death of my father, Dariush Shayegan became my lifesaver.

Farzan Rooz Publishing House was a great gathering place for Iranian intellectuals, and many showed up at the monthly meetings that I organized. Shayegan was surrounded by a few conservative men who did not like the radical tone of the lectures and conferences. Many of the intellectuals I invited were blacklisted, and I finally joined their ranks on a hot summer day in 1995 when one of my Iranian publishers called me and told me that the Ministry of Culture and Islamic Guidance had sent them a letter asking them not to publish my books. We were under close surveillance at Farzan and occasionally had informal visits from security officers who sat in the audience during our monthly meetings.

These were years of living dangerously. In the summer of 1995 there had been an unsuccessful attempt to kill a busload of writers en route to a poetry conference in Armenia. This incident was followed by the unexplained deaths of dozens of intellectuals, scholars, writers, and journalists opposed to the regime. I knew many of them and, according to a close friend, I was probably a soft target myself. My collaboration with the French Institute for Iranian Studies (IFRI), headed by the archaeologist Rémy Boucharlat, and my having invited intellectuals and writers like Paul Ricoeur and V.S. Naipaul to Iran in 1995 and 1996 put me at risk. I continued to collaborate with several journals, including *Kyan*, *Negah-No*, *Donyay-e Sokhan* and especially *Goftegu*, which I had founded with Morad Saghafi, Kaveh Bayat, and Zarir Merat in 1993. *Goftegu* was a critical quarterly that we intended to be an Iranian version of the literary magazines *Temps Modernes* and *Esprit*. The fact that most of us were French-speaking helped us establish the journal, and my past experiences with *Esprit* proved useful. *Goftegu* had its following among the younger generation of the Iranian elite and found many collaborators inside and outside Iran.

My intention in those years was to establish a bridge between the French and Iranian intelligentsia. To this end, in 1994 I invited Olivier Mongin, a French philosopher and the former director of *Esprit*, to Tehran to speak. My insatiable appetite for writing and intellectual work led me to work closely with other Iranian magazines and journals. Among these, *Kyan* was of a great interest because, unlike *Goftegu,* it brought together a group of religious thinkers, including Abdolkarim Soroush, Akbar Ganji, Arash Naraghi, Youssefi Eshkevari, and Mohsen Kadivar. Religious intellectuals in those years had in common a recognition of the need for reform in Islamic thought and a belief in democracy, civil society, religious pluralism, and opposition to the absolute supremacy of the *faqih* or Islamic law.

For the past two decades, Abdolkarim Soroush has been trying to persuade his fellow citizens that it is possible both to be Muslim and to believe in democracy. He stresses that there are two views of religion, a maximalist and a minimalist one. In the maximalist view, according to him, everything has to be derived from religion, and most of the current problems in Islam come from this belief. But the minimalist view implies that some values, such as respect for human rights, cannot be derived from religion. For Soroush, the maximalist view has to be supplanted by the minimalist; otherwise, a balance between Islam and democracy will not be possible. A democratic Islamic society would not need any Islamic norms imposed from above.

I agree with Soroush, although I think that Iranian society has become more secularized than he realizes. Secularism in Iran has become a set of moral values for governance. It is an organizing principle of social life, and it has opened up a non-religious, though fundamentally spiritual, space in the public sphere. It has also brought about changes to traditional political culture, among them a culture of dissent among women, intellectuals, and youth. The new generation was not around or is too young to remember the Revolution, but it made up one-third of eligible voters in the 2013 presidential election. The rebellious youth movement that has emerged in recent years is increasingly part of a larger global cultural movement. Subversive practices such as men and women mixing socially, free love, the makeover of the hijab as a fashion item, and the rise of secular ideals among religious intellectuals are all visible forms of secularism in the public sphere. More specifically, Iranian youth have challenged the established equation of the religious self with the Iranian self and have elaborated an alternative Iranian self. Life for young Iranians is not easy, but they manage to live it in an extraordinarily vibrant way, facing everyday dangers that breed creativity and rebelliousness. In comparison to the life of a young Iranian, which resembles a permanent struggle for creativity, living in a country like Canada, proud of its health care, security, and optimism, seems to me the best way to end up with an uncreative and boring future. Strangely, while many young men and women in North America fill up the mosques, churches, temples, and synagogues, in Iran the mood is to think about spirituality outside the terms of organized religion. As a result, the secular has become part of how many young Iranian Muslims understand themselves and their national identity.

Iranian youngsters have learned to live a double life: in public they conform to Islamic regulations and norms and in private they live in an underground cultural world they have created. Many who grew up after the Iranian Revolution suffer from a James Dean syndrome—they are fierce rebels without a cause. They don't know where to go or what to do and feel misunderstood and frustrated. In the mid-1990s, I found myself in the middle of two nations: an intolerant Iran of religious fanatics, organized criminals, and angry protesters of the kind we see on television brandishing "Down With America" placards, and an Iran of young people living a hedonistic life. For many of the latter, sex was both a motive for social rebellion and an act of political dissent. They risked their personal safety to meet friends, to go to parties and, ultimately, to have sex. Sexual experiences were a favourite topic and a marker of social success among these young Iranians.

Premarital and post-marital sex with multiple partners is increasingly common in Iran, although it remains culturally taboo and punishable under the law. But no amount of repression from the Iranian regime has curtailed the changes in sexual behaviour, which have done far more to reshape the country's cultural and political values than the political and intellectual revolts of the past thirty years. In those years in Tehran, I never faced the whip and I managed to dodge arrest on several occasions—I had no idea that one day I would find myself in an even worse situation.

MY THOUGHTS WERE interrupted by the sound of the heavy steel door to my cell opening. It was one of the older jailers bringing the evening meal. Prison food was mediocre, so I was concerned about keeping in good physical condition. I was still not sleeping well and my back ached every morning from sleeping on concrete. However, I did not want to give in to feelings of hopelessness and despair so, from the very first days of my detention, I spent at least two hours a day exercising. It was a physical reaction to the psychological pressure of solitary confinement and intense interrogations, during which I was seated and blindfolded. I planned my exercises based on what I could remember of the yoga lessons I had taken in the 1990s in Tehran. I quickly found out how difficult it is to concentrate on exercise in a tiny prison cell, but I learned to take my spirit out of the prison. Sometimes just looking at the Dalai Lama's photo, which I found in the pages of Gandhi's *Autobiography* that my wife had brought me, gave me the feeling that I was in his presence in the Himalayas. The book was a blessing. It helped me transform my hope of survival into the survival of hope.

Solitary confinement encourages the triumph of death over life and, in the case of Iranian prisons, of mediocrity and ignorance over nobility of thought. It reveals the limits of one's ethical paradigms. Its dehumanization took me into what Primo Levi calls "a gray zone," where there are no firm boundaries between innocence and guilt, good and evil, and the human and the inhumane. To avoid thinking about this confusion, I read Gandhi and his clear distinction between the violent and nonviolent, between the human and inhumane.

While I was reading, I felt that Gandhi was whispering in my ears: "Try your own experiments with truth." I thought alongside him and about his concepts without wanting to imitate him. In writing about his life, he took to heart Socrates' adage, "The unexamined life is not worth living." I have always considered his Socratic experiments with truth as among the great moments of self-realization of human consciousness. I was interested in Gandhi not only as a prophet of nonviolence or as a legendary leader but as a human being, with all the strengths and weaknesses that humans share. There is a Shakespearean dimension to his life, for he knew he could not remake the world and yet had the courage to press for nonviolent change. Reading Gandhi in the silence of my cell, far from civilized life, helped me accept the limits of my own ambition to change the world.

7

THERE IS JUST ONE STEP FROM INTOLERANCE TO cruelty, and people take this step all too easily. We all have the potential to do evil, to dehumanize and harm others. We think that a wall as solid as rock separates us from barbarism, but for those incapable of choosing between compassion and hatred, the separation is as thin as air. A touch here, a push there, and the stage is set for evil. The inhumane anywhere is a threat to humanity. As Martin Luther King Jr. says, "The bell of man's inhumanity to man does not toll for any one man. It tolls for you, for me, for all of us."

My growing belief that our differences should not prevail over our shared humanity was consolidated by my confinement. Yet it was precisely these differences that were fixed in the minds of my interrogators, passed down from their superiors. According to their rigid black-and-white way of thinking, there are some in the world who, because of their religion or ethnicity, automatically pose a political or cultural threat to the Islamic Republic.

After I was moved to my new cell, where I kept myself busy reading Gandhi's *Autobiography* and writing my thoughts on scraps of tissue and biscuit boxes, the tone of my daily interrogation changed: my persecutors believed they had discovered damning evidence of my guilt. As usual, I was blindfolded and made to sit for hours facing the wall, while my interrogators sat behind me.

"Why do you have so many Jewish friends, Mr. Jahanbegloo?" one of them asked, his tone dead serious, yet betraying a tinge of irony.

"What do you mean? I've had many colleagues and acquaintances throughout my years in academia and outside it, and some of them happen to be Jewish."

"Yes, but too many of them are Jewish," he said.

"I have no idea what you mean. I don't see what their religion or ethnicity has to do with it. As I've tried to tell you, we are all scholars; our job is to educate." I knew what he was going to say next.

"Merely to educate? No, I don't believe that's it at all. You claim that you want to educate, but educate whom and for what? Look at this list of your past associates— Isaiah Berlin, George Steiner, Noam Chomsky, and all these others. You think we don't know who these people are and what they do? They are all dangerous thinkers, and they all have an agenda."

"If you actually read the writings of those men, you'd know how wrong you are," I said, immediately regretting it.

"Oh, so you think you have all the knowledge here? You have all the right interpretations and we know nothing? Watch how you speak to me. I've only been this kind to you because you have cooperated up to this point, but if you start to get aggressive with us, believe me it won't turn out well for you. We have many other methods to employ."

A dead silence. They hadn't tortured me physically, but there was nothing to stop them.

"All I was trying to say is that there are different ways of understanding the writings of certain thinkers, and you have chosen to see them in one particular way. If you look at them another way, they may not seem as harmful as you think."

"Who are you to decide what is harmful or not? Have you not written papers in support of the Zionists?"

"Of course not," I replied. "What do you mean?"

"Look at this article here, for example, about your visit to Auschwitz. Do you not realize that in writing this article you have criticized the president's views and given the Zionists credibility?"

Ahmadinejad was and is a Holocaust denier. The paper I had written spelled out the fact that millions of Jews had been killed by the Nazis and that the death camp at Auschwitz was a centre of inhumanity and cruelty.

"But I never refer in any place to the president and his views. I wrote about a place that I visited and saw with my own eyes, and I wrote about my reaction to it."

"Yes, and in so doing you give ammunition to the Zionists to legitimize their claims and strengthen their grip over those they oppress. Have you ever been to Israel, Mr. Jahanbegloo?" he asked, his tone implying that he already knew the answer.

"I . . . when I was a child, yes. I couldn't have been more than five or six years old. I remember only the huge grapefruits on the trees."

"Well, you're not a child anymore, so don't play games with me. Even if you haven't been back since, you've been in contact with Israelis. You've supported their regime all your life."

"That's not true at all. I also had many Palestinian friends when I was in France. I knew Edward Said. I even organized a conference at Tehran University in his honour after his death."

"Not all Palestinians are true revolutionaries! The ones with whom you've been in contact are complicit in the

Zionists' wrongdoing because they don't confront it with full force. They may as well be on their side."

"They are different kinds of revolutionaries—" I started to say.

"Enough! No more of these quick answers. You still have not explained why you've written these articles about the Holocaust, why you side with the Zionists in all matters, why you insist on seeing them as the victims."

He was right. I hadn't given him an adequate account, for I knew he would not understand. How could I explain that my main concern was with inhumanity, how pervasive it is and how preventable, when he was already caught in its vise? The Islamic radicals had persecuted certain ethnic and religious minorities in Iran since the beginning of the revolution. Many members of minorities in Iran have faced discrimination for decades.

One prominent case, which set the tone for this injustice, was that of Habib (Habibollah) Elghanian, a prominent Iranian Jewish businessman and philanthropist who served as the president of the Tehran Jewish Society and was the leader of the Iranian Jewish community in the 1970s. In 1959, Elghanian established Plasco, a plastics manufacturing factory, which grew to become the largest and most technologically advanced plastics manufacturer in Iran. He was among the few who introduced modern Western technology to Iran in the 1960s and 1970s, and he built Tehran's first high-rise building. A multi-millionaire, Elghanian was widely respected for his business accomplishments and for his philanthropy in both Iran and Israel. On May 9, 1979, he was executed by a firing squad in Tehran after being convicted of espionage. His death and the seizure of all of his belongings shocked the Jewish community and many promptly fled Iran. He was the first Jew and one of the first civilians to be executed by the new Islamic government.

I never met Mr. Elghanian and I was never interested to meet rich men like him, but I happened to go to *Taraneh-No* primary school with Steve Elghanian, a relative of his. I had several classmates from other countries and other religions but I didn't notice any differences among us. I never distinguished between Ali and David, or between Hassan and Daniel. Steve and I studied together, ate together, played together, and went to the same parties. He was not one of my best friends, who were a Jewish boy named Isaac and a Zoroastrian friend, Goshtasb Vafadari. For most of us those were years of peace and happiness. We had no idea that one day the wheel of history would turn and we would encounter fear and hatred. I knew who my friends were and why they were my friends. And I was not alone. No one who believes in shared fate can feel hatred for another person. However, my interrogators wanted to make me believe that friendship with a

Jew or a Baha'i was a curse. They wanted me to draw a line that separated me from my Jewish friends. Things seemed to them to be either one way or another, or rather their way or no way at all. People, especially those without the ability to think, often fail to comprehend their own potential for inhumanity. Some unquestioningly take that small step into cruelty. But one wins in life not for being the stronger but for being the more just. As Pascal says, "Might without justice is tyrannical."

Why do cruelty and inhumanity happen? Why had I looked to Auschwitz for the answers? Auschwitz is not an unknown in Iran. Most educated Iranians have heard about it and know that it was an infamous place where Jews were killed en masse. But not many Iranians have the urge to visit it. Even those who go to Poland to study or do business rarely visit Auschwitz. I went to Auschwitz in February 2004 during a trip to Poland to meet with intellectuals and artists for a special issue of an Iranian journal. After meeting the poet and Nobel Prize winner Wislawa Szymborska in Krakow, I decided to take a taxi to the site of the death camp. It was a cold afternoon and I was among the last visitors allowed in. I was terrified by the idea of what I was going to see. As the car drew near, I could see a single railway line, disappearing into a red-brick building—the terminus of the line to Aus-chwitz-Birkenau built in the spring of 1944. Barbed wire and brick barracks stretched as far as the eye could see. The ruined crematoriums were nearby, all covered with a layer of snow. Seeing Auschwitz under the purity of freshly fallen snow heightened the barbarity of the place, and it seemed almost inconceivable that it was a creation of rational, modern minds.

Many years ago I read the memoirs of some survivors, including Primo Levi's *Survival in Auschwitz* and Elie Wiesel's *Night*, but the direct experience of the horror of the extermination camp goes beyond the power of words to express or even the imagination to conceive. Being imprisoned there was the most horrible experience anyone could ever survive.

Visiting Auschwitz is not like visiting any other prison camp or torture chamber. The horrifying expression of human cruelty and madness would certainly be as shocking, but what makes Auschwitz unique is not only the shock it elicits from seeing its assembly line of death but the bitter taste it leaves of disgust with mankind, which remains with you forever. The most important lesson of Auschwitz is not that the Holocaust was an evil and catastrophic event in Jewish and modern history but that it is a challenge to human existence. The murder of millions of innocent human beings is not an ordinary crime; of the more than eleven million who died in Nazi concentration camps, at least a million were gassed or died of other causes in Auschwitz. The Holocaust is the failure of ethics and an aberration from the fundamentals of civilization because it is the unlimited degradation and destruction of the human condition.

Presenting the meaning of Auschwitz in words is not possible even for poets, philosophers, and politicians. Auschwitz is an unbelievable expression of inhumanity and it is our responsibility today to witness the atrocity of Auschwitz in order to buttress the humane. The Holocaust is a moral outrage that goes beyond the comprehension of the individual mind, but moral discourse can still describe and evaluate the barbarities practiced by the Nazis. The best moral challenge to the Holocaust is never to forget that it happened and that it could happen again. The true lesson of Auschwitz is not about the past but about the future and about creating opportunities for dialogue and cooperation between cultures and religions. The true lesson of the Holocaust is that even "civilized" people are capable of atrocities and monstrosities, and the capacity to avoid thinking about them exists in all of us.

While trying to convey this idea to my interrogators, I realized that they had an essential quality that distinguished them from me. They were hardened men—they had hardened themselves. I was reminded of what the main character in Andrei Tarkovsky's stunning movie

Stalker had to say of such men: "Let them have a laugh at their passions. Because what they call passion actually is not some emotional energy, but just the friction between their souls and the outside world. And most important, let them believe in themselves. Let them be helpless like children, because weakness is a great thing and strength is nothing . . . . Hardness and strength are death's companions. Pliancy and weakness are expressions of the freshness of being. Because what has hardened will never win."

I had not ossified my view of the world; my life experiences had not permitted me to. I was born in a Zoroastrian hospital. The doctor who helped bring me into the world was a Baha'i. I went to a primary school run by a Jew and later to high school in English. I have always been a traveller and travelling has given me a cosmopolitan vision. It permits human contact, real encounters with others that expose our similarities and bring to light our differences as things to be cherished, not lamented.

In Paris, I fell in love with a Jewish girl who taught English literature at Tel Aviv University and was a student of George Steiner. Steiner introduced me to her during his visit to Paris in the spring of 1992 where he was delivering a series of lectures he titled "The Origins of Artistic Oeuvre." His visit took place a few months after I had finished my book of conversations with him at Cambridge University. We were in a café near the

Pantheon when Shoshana came in. George invited her to our table and introduced me as the co-author of the book of conversations. I learned that her father was an Iranian Jew who had fled Iran for Israel many years before the Iranian Revolution. We had fun that night, talking about writers, literature, and Jewish thinkers. I called her the next day and asked her out again. I wasn't sure about the future of my relationship with her. I knew that I had to leave Paris for Tehran shortly to be with my mother, who had asked me to join her after my father died. But I wanted to postpone going home by risking, by giving, by losing, as good things happen only to those who have the courage to lose sight of the shore. We were attracted to each other—that was obvious—but we each knew that our countries separated us, not because we believed in the intolerances that kept them apart but because we were both victims of other people's prejudices. Why should individuals pay for the hatred that is perpetrated by governments? This is the unsolved enigma of history. Our relationship turned out to be a shared joy and we brought out the best in each other. We saw each other every day. I rarely had this kind of relationship with a woman, someone with whom I could share both friendship and love. Now I realize that, like Rick and Ilsa in *Casablanca*, what we really had was Paris. Mostly I remember the last time I saw her. We were on a station platform feeling sad because I was leaving for Tehran. I knew I would not see her again. It was October 15, 1992, and I never heard from her again.

8

THE SMELL IS THE FIRST THING THAT HITS YOU
when you enter prisons in Iran. Since prisoners are supposed to make no noise, they become more sensitive to
smells. I encountered the Evin Prison smell each time I
had to walk down the long corridors to the interrogation
room. Ironically, most of the prisoners in Iranian prisons don't comment much about smell, or say they can't
smell anything. But I think that section 209, which is the
less-populated part of Evin Prison, had the smell of a five-
day sweat. With the exception of the everyday smell of
the prison, to which a prisoner gets accustomed, an occa-
sional smell would open a whole universe of memories to
me. Smell is a magic potion that can transport a person a
thousand miles away from solitary confinement. Sometimes while sitting in my cell and lost in my thoughts the
sudden smell of rosewater, which is frequently used in Iran

as a perfume, would bring back memories of my maternal grandmother's room. For as long as I can remember, my maternal grandmother had used rosewater; I can't smell rosewater without thinking of her. She was the epitome of an Iranian lady of the 1930s, always well-dressed and very distinguished. I cannot remember any scent she wore, but I associate many smells with her room. She lived with us for a long time and each time I entered her room I had the feeling of being a perfect *flaneur* in the middle of a Persian Bazaar. Balzac described *flânerie* as "the gastronomy of the eye," but it might also be a "gluttony of smell." It is fantastic how ephemeral scents evoke a sense of the remembrance of an instant. I rejoiced in the power of the scents in my grandmother's room, like a prince walking incognito through an oriental perfume shop. These brief flashes of scent and hints of feeling, now many years gone, reminded me of what was beautiful and serene. I missed these smells every single day that I sat in my cell.

Prisons, unlike women, never smell mysterious. When we lean toward a woman and close our eyes and inhale her perfume, it is like happiness. How can we wear happiness without pouring a few drops on other people? Coco Chanel once said, "A women who doesn't wear perfume has no future." Political prisoners may not be allowed to wear perfumes, but they think of the future every day. Hope is the perfume of the prisoner. If you continue smelling it, it can give you energy. It is like the first swallow of water after you have just crossed the desert. The day a prisoner stops hoping is the day he dies. His soul has been executed. But in prison I came to a crossroad in my life and knew I had to choose the right path, a path of principle that leads to integrity. I had my future in my hands. I could not choose where I came from, but I could choose where I would go in the future. All I had, sitting in my prison cell, were the choices that I made. It is ironical; I met my destiny on the road I took to avoid it. There must be a reason that I was where I was. This was my destiny and I held it in the palm of my hands. I measured my moments, I measured my steps. It is the eternal right of every man to fight against his fate. I remembered a quote from Stanley Kubrick's *A Clockwork Orange*, "When a man cannot choose, he ceases to be a man." In the long run we all have to make tragic choices in life in order to go on living. Sitting in a prison cell, I realized that one's life is the sum total of the choices not made. This is life's great paradox. Even God has no answer for the wasted years of life. For me, a life never tasted is forever wasted. And when I was in prison, I realized I wanted to taste every second of my life once I was free. Sleep in a bed, find some security, and be with someone who cares for me. Life is a gift that you never know how to use until you fight for it. Sitting alone, in my cell, I know that I have to measure every moment and count every step. And yet, I am not making any plans. I am just going to let life surprise me.

I hear one of the jailers behind my door. He opens the door and takes a good look at me sitting on the floor and sinking into my thoughts.

"It's time," he said. "Put on your blindfold and follow me to the interrogation room."

9

IN MID-JUNE, AFTER I WAS MOVED TO THE NEW cell, I was left alone for two weeks, abandoned even by my interrogators. The new cell contained a private toilet and a shower, so I no longer had to wait for a guard to take me to the toilet and could take showers twice a day. I went back to my usual washing habits and the hot water calmed my nerves. As the summer heat breathed through the window below the ceiling of my cell, I lay on the concrete floor wondering what had happened. Had I been too obstinate? Were they getting impatient with me? Was I not telling them everything they wanted to know? No answers came, no one came, and for the next weeks I had no contacts except with my interrogators.

Books became my only companions. I passed the long, desolate hours reading books my wife had brought to the prison for me: Gandhi, Nehru, and Hegel. They all helped me to forget the grim present. Since childhood, I have been obsessed and fascinated by books. Like Jorge Luis Borges, I consider them an absolute necessity. As he famously said, he imagined Paradise in the form of a library. For good readers, under normal circumstances, books enrich life, injecting passion and enchantment into the mundane and quotidian.

In solitary confinement, books help you to survive: you can never underestimate their power and importance in such a place. Oddly, Hegel's abstract philosophy proved to be best at pulling my mind out of the horrible dungeon in which I was living. Never in the many years that I had read and taught Hegel's *Phenomenology of Spirit* had I experienced such intimacy with a philosophy in the making. In my cell I would read each paragraph out loud so that I could hear the sound of his abstract concepts. I felt as if I was part of his epic voyage of philosophical discovery; that I was a stage in the spiritual evolution he writes about.

Phenomenology became my inseparable companion, especially at night when the prison was haunted by a frightening silence. Sitting on my blanket on the cold floor, I would take this huge book in my hands and start reading it slowly and quietly aloud, so that only I could hear my voice. Sentences such as "Universal freedom can ... produce neither a positive achievement nor a deed; there is left for it only negative action; it is merely the rage and fury of destruction" made my suffering soul tremble with excitement. Wasn't I a victim of this tendency towards destruction, combined with an unyielding and constant suspicion, which leads inevitably, after each revolution in history, to the killing of innocents? I was sharing the same fear that so many had felt before their execution.

Evin Prison has the task not only of crushing life but also of wiping out the individuality that threatens everything that the Iranian Revolution espouses. Every act that springs from individuality is treated as a crime and its perpetrator assumed to be guilty—a guilt that only confession followed by death can absolve. The lesson that I saw in this was simple: a revolution is capable only of condemnation, and the guilty party, like me, must either negate the revolution or be negated by it. I also understood that revolutions produce political mechanisms and judicial structures that are supposed to destroy individuals, not protect them. The tree of revolution must be refreshed from time to time with the blood of innocents. Revolutions and their laws cannot forgive, only human beings can. This understanding of forgiveness is the greatest lesson that I've learned from reading books.

There are times in our lives when our inspiration comes from a space beyond words. We find ourselves relying upon something other than the five senses or the sheer rules of logic. I have this feeling each time I read a great book in my life. Books have affected the way I look at everything, from the concept of freedom to the question of God. Saint-Exupéry's *The Little Prince* was the first book to completely blow my mind. When I was ten it opened my eyes to the power of ideas and the joy of reading. It ignited my imagination as no other had done before. It was the first time I had felt such a bond with a character; I saw values in *The Little Prince* that I wanted to emulate in my own life. The main character's decision to leave his star and travel to various planets, seeking answers to life's questions, triggered a voyage of discovery in my own life. At that age I could not understand what life was really about, but I could feel the significance of the book's last words: "But the eyes are blind. One must look with the heart." From books I have learned how to travel from star to star to discover that I am not alone and to learn to see with my heart.

I have always felt nostalgic for the books I read during my adolescent years, books I could never read again with the same pure and innocent eyes. Like many authors, I am a creature of libraries: I can trace my life through the books I have read. The story of the book is synonymous with the story of libraries; the reflections and histories of men and women throughout history are contained in them. The greatness of Western, Chinese, Indian, and

Islamic civilizations is recorded in their libraries, not in the individual, ephemeral biographies of their citizens. Two forces in history have successfully influenced the education of cultivated man: art and philosophy. Both are united in libraries. A library is not merely a space where books are shelved but a storehouse of ideas, where every piece of wisdom from the world's past and present is available on request.

What does it mean to love libraries? It means to take them as an introduction to the cornerstones of human civilization. I rarely enter a library without feeling a shiver of reverence, without appreciating the traces left in its books by men and women of the past.

I grew up with three libraries at home: mine, my father's, and my mother's. Later, while I lived in Paris, I built up my own library over a period of twenty years. It was more an intellectual exercise than anything else. Before I knew it I had almost a thousand books, which were shelved all over my tiny apartment.

Arranging books is an art that needs time and spirit. Some people arrange books by topic, others by author, some even by colour. I had friends who stacked their books randomly, piling them horizontally onto shelves. One of my classmates had the idea of stopping his library at 365 books; his plan was to have one book for each day of the year. I found great pleasure in adding different topics to my collection, which soon led to the problem of too many books for the size of my apartment. I did not have the good fortune of Captain Nemo, who says in *Twenty Thousand Leagues Under the Sea*, "But I was done with the shore the day my *Nautilus* submerged for the first time under the waters. That day I bought my last volumes, my last pamphlets, my last newspapers, and ever since I've chosen to believe that humanity no longer thinks or writes." Books occupied my entire apartment: they were in the living room, the bedroom, and the entranceway. I even had books in my bathroom, though it was not my favourite place to read. I constantly moved them from one room to another, from one shelf to another, one pile to another. I could spend hours looking for a book without finding it, but without regret, as living among books is like being Don Juan in a harem.

I was under the delusion that a library could never be lost or destroyed. But we all know that books are feared by dictators and fanatics alike; it would take a very long time to compile a list of all the libraries destroyed by tyrannies and wars. The loss of the library at Alexandria was a particularly grievous blow to civilization.

I sold my Paris apartment in 1997, when I went to live in Canada, and a twenty-year chapter of my life as a young man and a student closed. I was naive enough to listen to the advice of a real estate agent, by the name of

Ruhi, who wanted to sell my apartment before the beginning of the Eurozone in 1999. As we closed the deal, she promised to keep my books safe, in a cellar, in return for a sum of money. Two years later, after my divorce, on a trip to Paris, I called her and asked about my books. I had learned from someone else that she had sold them to second-hand bookshops; now she pretended that the job had been done by someone who had since left France for Tunisia. I was so furious and devastated that, sitting in a café, I cried for two hours. I was reminded of the 1935 novel by Elias Canetti entitled *Auto-da-Fé* (*Die Blendung* in its original title) about Professor Peter Kien, a leading Sinologist, whose most cherished possession is his great library. His cloistered life is shattered when he decides to marry his illiterate and grasping housekeeper, who eventually robs him of everything. The novel ends with the protagonist burning himself alive in his library because he cannot deal with the mediocrity of his time.

Among the cherished books I lost were those signed by writers I knew personally. One was the 1969 book by Isaiah Berlin, *The Four Essays on Liberty*, which he signed for me when we first met in June 1988. After ten years, I ceased to believe the book had survived; I even ceased mourning the loss of my precious library. Then something happened, almost like a fairy tale come true. One day I received an email from Robert Quick, a dealer in second-hand and scarce books, who told me he had a book by Isaiah Berlin, signed to me. I wrote back and explained that the book had been stolen from my library. A few days later Robert responded by giving me more details about the book:

"I bought the book from a used book shop in the Finchley area of London several years ago. I paid seven pounds and did not notice the inscription until a few months ago. Please understand my caution as I've learned that fraudulent claims of ownership of books are fairly common. Assuming that you are, in fact, the Ramin Jahanbegloo to whom Dr. Berlin inscribed the book, I can appreciate your desire to have it back and would be willing to get it to you. I'd be willing to send the book to original owner—with adequate proof."

I sent him proof of my identity and a cheque to cover the postage and the price of the book, and soon I had two copies: the one signed for me by Berlin and another, which I'd bought after losing hope of ever recovering my lost book.

I often dream that before I die a day will come when I can see all my books gathered in one place again. This, however, was difficult to imagine while I was sitting in a cell and hoping to put together my divided self by reading Hegel.

Later, Nehru's autobiography kept me company. I could

relate to his prison experience, down to the last visceral detail. Even the insects in my cell took on a special significance after I read that, during his imprisonment, he had also been irritated by them. Glad to have evidence of life going on, as annoyed as I was with cockroaches and ants, I looked at them as reminders of Nehru's invisible company. When I finally lost my patience with them, I covered the floor with newspaper. The only paper I was allowed to have was *Kayhan*, a conservative paper, which published articles denouncing me and other reformist Iranian intellectuals. I wanted to laugh that I was allowed such reading, though no laughter ever came.

To alleviate my loneliness and depression, I read Nehru's words out loud. I needed to hear a human voice, even if it was my own. At one point the guards grew suspicious of my activities—talking to myself, scattering newspapers everywhere, and covering the floor—so they came in, blindfolded me, and searched the cell. They discovered the bag in which I kept my notes and aphorisms, written on scraps of torn-up boxes, and confiscated everything immediately. The experience left me exhausted.

I finally deduced why the interrogations had stopped when I heard cheering and shouting coming from the guards' quarters. It was the unmistakeable sound of football fans and I realized that the World Cup had been going on and must now be close to the final stages. I listened intently, trying to figure out who was playing, but the indistinct yells provided no clues. I had been a big football fan during my teenage years, and later, even with my busy academic schedule at the Sorbonne, I never missed a World Cup. Now I had to laugh over the ruckus being made about such a trivial thing as a game. What did football matter in solitary confinement? Nothing, I thought—but that was before I learned an important lesson in human interaction.

I finally gathered the courage to speak to one of the guards when he brought me food. I had caught glimpses of him during the two months I had been there, but he'd never said anything to me except to issue instructions.

"Bring your plate to the slot," he said mechanically. I had seen him in parts through the slot in the steel door—his hands, his torso, sometimes his lower jaw and nose—but for the first time I saw his eyes. Words came to me, and I asked without thinking.

"Have you been following the football games?" I asked.

He hesitated for a moment as he filled the plate with food, then replied curtly, "Yes."

That was all that was needed: a simple, affirmative word; the acknowledgement of my existence by another living soul.

"Who's winning?" I asked, knowing he had to reply now.

"Argentina," he said, adding, after a pause, "but I think Germany will come back and win it."

"The Germans are resilient."

"Yes, tough players. They have character. Brazil is my favourite team though. I like their style of play."

"Few nations know football like the Brazilians. When I was younger, Pelé and Jairzinho were my idols. They were unstoppable, and even now nobody plays like them."

"Yes," he replied, now looking into my eyes through that tiny slot.

"So, who do you think will win the tournament?" I asked.

"If Germany comes back in this game, I think they have a good chance of going on to win it. But of course Brazil plays tomorrow against France, and I would never bet against them."

"Will you let me know the result?"

"I'm not sure if I'll be able to," he said. " I may not catch that game tomorrow."

I said nothing. I could see that he had opened himself up to me a little too much and was now embarrassed. He looked away and was about to leave.

"I think you're more of a prisoner than I am, then."

His eyes flashed for a moment as he turned to me again, but then he looked down as if suddenly understanding.

"I don't know how long I'll be here," I continued. "I'm on the other side of the bars. But you spend all your days here, giving food to prisoners like me."

I was surprised at myself for saying this, but I could see that he somehow accepted it.

"It's true," he said. "I, too, suffer."

He looked around a little, threw me another glance, and left without saying anything else—but ponderously, with slow, gentle steps, as if he did not want to disturb the fragility of this moment. I had touched a nerve, but he wasn't angry. We had merely had a brief human connection.

This was not the only time I made such a connection in prison. From time to time the resident barber cut my hair. He arrived one day, accompanied by a guard, and waited at the door as my blindfold was put on and I was taken into the corridor. I could see through a gap below the blindfold that he was wearing dark khaki pants and unpolished black dress shoes. He sat me on a single chair beside the door of my cell and gently put a cape around my neck while muttering to himself.

"Is this your job? You do this all the time?"

"Yes, yes," he replied in the voice of a tired old man. "Only for a few more months now, though. I used to be a tailor. But I had to close my shop and then I had no job."

"So how did you end up here? This is an unusual place to look for work."

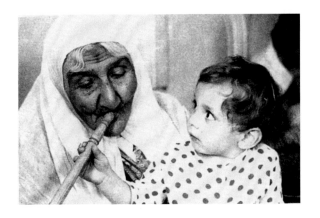

With my great-grandmother (age 101)
at my grandfather's house in Tehran, 1958.

*My father, Amir Hossein Jahanbegloo,
near the Caspian Sea, August 1957.*

*My mother, Khojateh Kia, in our house
in Tehran, November 1974.*

At the age of three,
Tehran, October 1959.

With my mother,
Tehran, April 1963.

*With my dogs at our house in the
north of Tehran, winter 1969.*

*My grandmother, Massomeh Samei, at
our house in Tehran, fall 1995.*

My daughter, Afarin, and my mother,
Istanbul, May 2012.

My mother, Khoji Kia, on her eightieth birthday, Kharagan, Iran, July 31, 2013.

With His Holiness the Dalai Lama,
Dharamsala, India, May 2007.

With Felipe González, former prime minister of Spain, at the World Political Forum, Turin, Italy, October 2009.

*With Jody Williams, Nobel Peace Prize
Laureate, at Forum 2000 Conference, Prague
Crossroads, Prague, September 2009.*

*With Václav Havel at Forum 2000
Conference, Prague Crossroads, Prague,
September 2009.*

*With Korean poet Ko Un and Nobel
Laureate Seamus Heaney at the First Milosz
Festival, Krakow, October 2009.*

With Rajmohan Gandhi, grandson of
Mahatma Gandhi, India, December 2010.

*With Roberto Toscano at Plaza de Oriente,
Madrid, July 2014.*

"By chance, just pure chance. My brother-in-law is a guard here, and he suggested it. He said I could come and go as I pleased, unlike the others who have to stay here all the time."

He told me a little more about his life as he went on cutting my hair and shaving me: he was married with two sons, one a soldier and one who worked in the bazaar. He was a firm and religious man. Eventually he grew quiet when he realized he was revealing too much about himself to a prisoner.

"So what are you in here for?" he finally asked.

"I've been accused of trying to start a soft revolution."

"Is that what you've done?"

"No, I'm innocent. I've done nothing wrong."

"Then God will help you," he said. "If you are innocent, then God will help you and you will get out."

I wanted to say that, whether God helped me or not, I was innocent all the same, but I stopped myself. Our fifteen minutes were over, and I had enjoyed talking with another human being; discussing religion would only complicate things. Back in my cell, I thought about those words we had exchanged and imagined what life would be like for an old man who worked as a barber in a horrid place like this just to make a living. I imagined going home to a wife and two sons, and wondered what their days would be like.

I longed for human company.

10

A FEW DAYS LATER I WAS PERMITTED TO MAKE A phone call. Immediately I called my wife and was glad to hear her voice when she answered. She was working out a deal to come for another visit, she told me. Excited, I asked if my mother would be able to come with her this time.

"Don't get too worried, but your mother's in the hospital, in the ICU," she told me, sounding sad and anxious. "Her blood pressure has gone up because of all the stress . . . of your situation. But she should be fine."

"I understand," I said. "I want to see her, but not like this. I don't want to put more pressure on her."

Visiting me would be very emotional for her. My mother is a strong woman, but my imprisonment was taking a toll; having gone through the same experience with my father, she could barely handle it. I felt guilty for having done this to her, as if I had purposely brought calamity down on both myself and those I love. So it was a fitting question that one of the guards asked, as he walked me back to my cell after the phone call: "Is it true that all philosophers are mad?"

"Not necessarily," I said. Then I added, "To be a philosopher is to have a critical view of all forms of conviction that end up in dogmatism."

He didn't understand my point. As he closed the cell door behind me, he said, "So, that means that you don't believe in God and Islam, and you are a heretic."

I was flabbergasted. But, then I remembered that if he had not thought like this, he would not be a guard at Evin. His judgment took me back to my years in France and my philosophy classes there.

I went to France in 1974 after graduating from Iranzamin Tehran International School in Tehran. I had decided to become a doctor and had applied to all possible pre-med colleges. My father was not sure where I should study, so I took the qualifying exams from several countries during my senior year in high school. I was admitted to two American universities, but my father decided to send me to France, so I left for Paris in September 1974. I had never travelled alone before, but I had lived apart from my parents in boarding schools in Switzerland and England. This time, it was different. I was barely eighteen and I was starting a new chapter in my life.

I was excited to see Paris again, a city I had visited in 1969 on my way to Algeria. The city for me was still represented by the student revolt of May 1968. I was picked up at the Orly airport by the cultural attaché of the Iranian embassy, who was a friend of my parents. He took me to the *Grand Hotel des Balcons* near the Place de l'Odéon. It was an old Parisian hotel in the Latin Quarter with small rooms and one shared bathroom on each floor. The hotel had a certain charm, but it was definitely not to everyone's taste. The important thing was that it was close to the Sorbonne and the Pantheon and it was less than a twenty-minute walk to the Seine and Notre-Dame Cathedral.

The first thing I did was to freshen up and rush to see all these places. Using the Sorbonne and the Odéon theatre as landmarks, I found myself at the site of the student riots of 1968. Farther on, in a little street off Boulevard Saint-Michel, I found Francois Maspero's bookstore, *La Joie de Lire*, commonly called *Chez Maspero*. My French was not good enough to read philosophy, but I could order breakfast and read French comic books. I couldn't contain myself when I entered Maspero's bookshop. It was late at night and youngsters and students were sitting all over the place reading. I saw a book on the Chinese Cultural Revolution with a picture of Red Guards on the cover. Coming from the Shah's Iran, where even Maxim Gorky and Bertolt Brecht's works were considered seditious, I was eager to read left-wing and radical literature. My father had never forced me to read political or religious books, and he had steered me away from ideas he knew the Shah's regime considered dangerous. I had started reading Marx's *Communist Manifesto* when I was in the tenth grade, after being introduced to it by one of my non-Iranian teachers. In any case, I wanted to know more about Mao Tse-tung and May '68, so I ended up buying three books on the French riots and the Chinese Cultural Revolution. These didn't suggest the first steps of a pre-med student.

Over the next few weeks I started to adapt to French society. I learned that I needed two years of pre-med before I took the entrance exam for medical school. My father had asked one of his students who was now living in Tours to look after me. Farhad was twelve years older than me and was an anti-Shah activist. A week after I arrived in Paris, where I was spending my days as a tourist, he came to my hotel and told me that he'd been asked by my father to take me in charge. The first thing he did was to take me to a party to meet left-wing, anti-Shah student activists who were in their thirties and forties. They found me too pampered for their taste and started giving me a lesson on Iranian politics. I read the leftist pamphlets they gave me, but I found them boring—most of them followed the Soviet Communist Party line, but showed no knowledge of Marxism. On weekends I would go to the student restaurant at Cité Universitaire, where all the anti-Shah groups gathered. There I met some students and activists who became leaders of political groups or famous intellectuals after the Revolution. However, I was too shy to engage in a proper conversation with any of them, especially because I found their delusion of revolutionary utopia frightening.

After a month in Paris, I decided to go to Tours to study advanced French and to register in a pre-med school. The Touraine is a lovely region in the heart of France, famed for its wine and for its chateaux, both of which I explored during my two-year stay. There I learned how to read and write literary French. I love French and deeply regret that it is no longer widely well-written or well-spoken. However, in the 1970s France had many great minds, and people both inside and outside the country held the language in great esteem. One of my classmates, Kenji, was a Japanese student who used to invite me home to his small room in a house owned by a bad-tempered French lady, where he served me Japanese food. Because of my conversations with him, I started reading Yukio Mishima and went to the small cinematheque to watch films by directors such as Ozu Yasujiro and Kenji Mizoguchi. Mishima became one of my favourite authors.

"I want to make a poem of my life," Mishima wrote when he was just twenty-four. He fulfilled his destiny on November 25, 1970, when he and four cadets took the commandant of the Japanese Self-Defence Force hostage. Mishima delivered a nationalist speech to the Japanese troops, intended to inspire a coup d'état. He said, in part, "We'll show you right now a value that is greater than the reverence for life. It's not freedom and it's not democracy. It's Japan, our beloved Japan, the land of history and tradition. Is there no one willing to die by hurling himself against the Constitution that has torn out the bones from what we hold dear? If there is, let him step forth. Even now let us rise together and die together." The soldiers did not listen to him and Mishima returned to the commandant's office and committed *seppuku*, ritual suicide. The act was a bizarre mixture of samurai warrior ritual and the expression of the aesthetic ideology he had developed. I admired Mishima's belief in a union of art and life, of literary style and heroic action, although I never wanted to imitate him. It would have been impossible to understand him fully outside Japanese culture. Nevertheless, he taught me to respect Japanese traditions.

I still think that artists like Mishima help us to understand life as an aesthetic gesture. It is widely held that Mishima wanted to pursue the lost legacy of the samurai code but actually, through the combination of literature and Japanese ritual suicide, the *seppuku*, he was mapping the synthesis of the sublime and the tragic. In looking back we can see the aesthetic strength of Mishima's action, which broke cultural boundaries. Behind his ritual suicide, one can find not only the beauty of death but also an unusual way of making one's life meaningful.

My friend Kenji had a private French teacher by the name of Brigitte. I met her at Kenji's and was so struck by her that I asked her to watch an Iranian movie at the cinematheque with me. We continued to see each other and our relationship eventually became more serious. Brigitte offered a window into a typical French lifestyle. Four years older and more experienced sexually than I was, she was studying to be a child psychologist. While I continued to go to my pre-med science classes at the University of Tours, where I had to memorize formulas and never ask questions, I began to audit some of Brigitte's classes. I was especially interested in animal behaviour. In my letters to my father I shared my enthusiasm for Konrad Lorenz and Rémy Chauvin. I was also introduced to Freud and started reading his works in English. That summer of 1975 everything seemed to guide me toward studying psychology, and I decided to become a doctor of the human soul rather than of the human body. But I was still trying to find my way.

My relationships with the Iranians I met in France were not good. In those days Iranians didn't need a visa for France, and young men from quite different family backgrounds found themselves together in small cities like Tours. The Iranians I met were not interested in learning more about French culture and spent most of their time playing cards or cooking Iranian dishes and listening to Iranian pop music. The political activists I met, for whom everything was either black or white, appalled me. The degradation of complexities into binaries is inevitable with political ideologies, but believers always lose sight of life's beautiful shades of grey. I was determined to keep my distance from all forms of prejudice and intolerance. At eighteen, nothing appeared to me as eternal or stable and I believed that everything can and must be renewed. I was learning to fight idolatry and tyranny, which can only lead to fear and slavish obedience. With Brigitte's help and the moral and financial support of my parents, I was able to take further steps toward my maturity.

Brigitte's father was an architect and a Freemason. He believed in France's civilizing mission and fully approved of its colonial occupation of Algeria and other countries. He didn't mind his daughter going out with me, a young man with a Muslim background, as long as I adopted French culture. Staying from time to time with Brigitte and her parents in their large home in the suburbs of Tours helped me learn their manners of eating and speaking, as well as their family values. I didn't agree with all aspects of the French mentality, including their egocentric thinking, which leads many to think that whatever they believe is necessarily true. But that didn't stop me from wanting to learn more about their culture.

Brigitte and her parents were nudists and they invited me to go with them to the island of Corsica. I thoroughly enjoyed my trip and was looking forward to my next adventure, which also opened new doors of perception for me. This was a trip to Greece in the fall of 1975. I was eager to visit the home of philosophy and the cradle of democracy. We went to Athens and the first place we visited was, of course, the Acropolis. Standing on the sacred rock, as the Greeks call it, where Paul first brought news of Jesus to the Greeks, I felt excited, overwhelmed, and humble all at once, thinking I was treading on the very same marble ground as Socrates and Plato and all the Sophist philosophers I had read about in Iran. Those few days in Greece sharply focused my awareness of what I wanted to do with my life.

My interest in psychology and Freud did not make me want to become a psychoanalyst. I was aiming at something more metaphysical and being in Greece helped me decide that philosophy was what could give full meaning to my life. I understood that the purpose of life is to live, and to live means to be aware, and one needs philosophy to be aware. From that day on, philosophy became my occupation. I struggled eagerly through books by Sartre and Camus, attended classes and lectures on philosophical matters, and cultivated the acquaintance of students of philosophy. My Iranian friend Farhad, with whom I had a constructive, if distant, relationship, introduced me to the works of Marcuse and Adorno. Susan Sontag was right to say, "A volume of Adorno's essays is equivalent to a whole shelf of books on literature." Reading his books was difficult but, as the years passed and I studied philosophy more deeply, I realized that Adorno, like many other philosophers, intended his readers to read his work attentively and thoughtfully. He and the other thinkers of the Frankfurt School made me understand that the true task of philosophy was to critique modern society and culture. By 1976, things were moving more quickly in my mind and in my life. I ended my relationship with Brigitte, who wanted us to get married and have children. I was at the beginning of my philosophical journey and not ready to settle down. She felt the pain of the breakup intensely and as a result I decided to go back to Paris. My parents had bought a small apartment at Rue Vavin, just opposite the famous restaurant *La Coupole*, and I lived there for the next fifteen years. I took courses in philosophy at the Catholic University and after that I got into the Sorbonne. By then I had the academic baggage of two years of science and three years of intense apprenticeship in psychology, philosophy, and French. I also had an experience that opened my mind in another way.

Since arriving in France, I had been reading what Sartre, Huxley, and the Beatnik writers had to say about their experiences with drugs. Both Huxley and Sartre brought a wide knowledge and understanding of philosophy and literature to their first psychedelic experiments and yet Huxley's experience was a revelation to him. In *The Doors of Perception*, he recounts his experience on mescaline at the height of its effect. Sartre's first drug experiment was also with mescaline, but he had a very bad trip and never took it again. After reading them, I started to think about taking LSD to discover its psychological effects for myself. One of my roommates had some experiences with drugs. He was a student at the Paris VIII University, known as Vincennes, established after May '68, where students could openly buy drugs like heroin and LSD. I asked him if he would watch over me during a trip on LSD. He agreed, and so, in December 1976, after a few months of struggling with my conscience and my fears, I took LSD. My trip was not good, though it had some interesting aspects. Everything around me lost meaning. Reality slipped from my grasp. I had no sense of time or space; everything was foreign and uncomfortable. I later realized that some LSD users kill themselves because they are never able to regain their sense of reality.

My roommate introduced me to a group of young, wealthy Iranians who were spending their time in Paris drinking, having sex, and taking drugs. We started going to rock concerts together, but I stopped after reading Adorno's 1938 essay "On the Fetish-Character in Music and the Regression of Listening," in which he talks about a massive regression both in listening and in all modes of aesthetic appreciation. His discussion of Mahler as a composer who is wholly against bourgeois taste, and therefore one whose works resist commodification, brought me back to classical music. I also stopped taking recreational drugs. I had not taken them to escape reality but to understand why human civilization allows its gift of poetic and philosophical transcendence to be supplanted by the hallucinatory visions offered by mind-altering drugs. My brief experience with drugs was a craving for the absolute. When I look back, I see it as a pure philosophical quest.

I have always considered philosophy as an encounter with the naked reality of the human mind and its majestic potential to make thinking a great adventure. My father gave me a taste for philosophy; life provided the education. My first philosophical experiences were merely a process of conditioning through the accumulation of information. But they still lacked the genuine, rational comprehension of things that goes hand in hand with a process of maturation. When I started studying philosophy at the

Sorbonne in the late 1970s, few believed that philosophy could play a critical role in the contemporary world. Many people used the term "philosophy," as in "philosophy of business" or "philosophy of a television program," without necessarily understanding what philosophy is. To my mind, philosophy is the most analytic and synthetic mode of thinking that humans have yet devised.

Today, philosophy is loosely associated with a form of idle speculation, and philosophers are looked at as academic bookworms whose knowledge deals with intangible ideas that do not contribute to the comforts or material progress of societies. Dictatorial regimes have always considered philosophy to be a subversive mode of thinking and a corruptor of youthful minds. That is what Socrates was convicted of, and that is why the Socratic task remains the main goal for many philosophers. When I started studying philosophy, many in the West lionized Lenin, Trotsky, Mao, and Che Guevara. Socrates was my hero for the reason Cicero pinpointed: "Socrates brought philosophy down from the skies." I chose this as my goal too: to continue the task of making philosophy central to improving our lives.

I loved all my philosophy classes at the Sorbonne. To me they represented the Athenian Agora, where Socrates asked the fundamental questions of human existence: What makes us happy? What makes us good?

What is virtue? What is love? How should we best live our lives? Among my professors, there were many who had conservative views. The most well-known among them was Pierre Boutang, who was a fervent supporter of the ideas of Charles Maurras. Like Maurras, Boutang was a royalist, who argued for the restoration of Christian monarchies and was loyal to the Comte de Paris. I considered Boutang a reactionary but I admired his knowledge of Pascal, Kierkegaard, and Aquinas. Other professors, among them Michel Haar, Maurice Birault, and Pierre Aubenque, were either followers or had been students of Martin Heidegger. I studied Nietzsche with Haar, Heidegger with Birault, and Aristotle with Aubenque. Though I disagreed politically with many of them, I was never bored in any of their classes.

In one of my first classes with Haar, he told us, "I envy you because not only are you young but you also have the courage to choose philosophy in an anti-philosophical world." For those of us who took philosophy seriously, there could not have been any other way. Philosophy is not a discipline with which you can have a one-night affair. It involves the thoughtful examination of concepts, principles, values, and practices that carry three thousand years of cultural, political, social, and religious influences. It demands a willingness to continually reflect and transform oneself, to be open to new ways of thinking, and to be unhappy with simplistic answers to basic questions about life.

I have studied the lives and thoughts of the great philosophers for more than thirty years, and I found that what motivates these men and women is the courage to use their own reason. Kant once said that in philosophy we are interested in three great questions: What can I know? What should I do? What may I hope? These three, however, can be subsumed under one great question: What is a human being? After all, the question of what a human being is would be inadequately answered without addressing the insoluble tension between wanting to know and yet being unable to know. The tragic nature of humanity, but also its way out of madness, is to know that not everything can be known. Philosophy has to live with this conflict; it is the philosophical condition of humankind.

Living in Paris helped me to develop my philosophical quest. On my way to study at the Sorbonne, I often crossed the Jardin du Luxembourg, a large park with a pond at its centre, where children sail model boats, and a fenced-in area with a playground, a merry-go-round, pony rides, and a puppet theatre. For years my reading of Plato, Spinoza, Kant, Hegel, and Nietzsche was accompanied by the sounds of Luxembourg. After my classes, I would sit for hours in *Café Rostand* in front of the park and write my essays while watching people pass by. Parisians take their café culture seriously; the idea of grabbing a Starbucks coffee to go is unthinkable. People sit at tables, side by side, and enjoy watching people walk by. I lived for twenty years in the Montparnasse neighbourhood, which is famous for its cafés and restaurants. Some of them were meeting places for authors and artists living in Paris—including Modigliani, Hemingway, and Picasso, whose studio was not far from my apartment. For many years my apartment in Paris was the centre for political and philosophical meetings. My Iranian friends, who were each studying a different subject (sociology, medicine, journalism, etc.), gathered at 47 Rue Vavin for discussions on anarchism, socialism, art, philosophy. We were all passionate about the Iranian Revolution and the election of Francois Mitterand as the new French president. I remember well the night of the second round of presidential elections when we joined our French socialist comrades and went to celebrate the victory of the French Left at the Bastille.

I also used to meet my classmates at Café Select to talk about politics and philosophy while hoping to see Sartre, Beckett, Ionesco, or Baudrillard, who lived in the same area of the city. Over an espresso or a glass of beer we made plans to start philosophy journals or to carry out protests in support of prisoners in Iran. Among this group of students, there were two whom I found particularly interesting: a

Jew by the name of Alain Douchevsky, who admired Max Stirner, and a Lebanese Christian, Kamal Yazigi, who had worked with George Habash and the Popular Front for the Liberation of Palestine during the 1975–77 civil war in Beirut. Kamal and I were great admirers of Schopenhauer and his philosophy and, as he was not very popular among those who read philosophy, we decided to start a Schopenhauer Society. I was the society's president and we held meetings at my apartment. I travelled to Germany to gather more documents on Schopenhauer and discovered that there was already a Schopenhauer Society in Frankfurt, which had many more activities than we had in mind. We abandoned the project but continued to be interested in Schopenhauer's thought, and the two of us did our Master's theses on his philosophy. Kamal also wrote his PhD on Schopenhauer while I switched to his contemporary and enemy, Hegel. I worked on Hegel and the French Revolution and started following the night seminars held by Pierre-Jean Labarrière, the great Jesuit specialist and Hegel translator. I have never felt so close to the essence of philosophy. Labarrière's line-by-line explanation of Hegel was like the taste of a great wine. It is easy to tell a good wine from a bad wine but hard to tell good wines apart. Labarrière's Hegel classes had the great taste of a 1961 Château Margaux. Later I learned that Jesuits are renowned for their unrelenting pursuit of science and philosophy. Labarrière not only taught us Hegelian concepts but was able to hand down Hegel's wisdom and his experience of life. This was his great achievement and what I learned from it has been a huge help to me in both studying and teaching philosophy.

In the early 1980s, while I was at the Sorbonne, Kamal introduced me to the work of Cornelius Castoriadis. Kamal had read Castoriadis while he lived in Beirut and was in contact with him. He asked me to accompany him to Castoriadis's class at the Ecole des Hautes Etudes. I am glad I did. I became so interested in Castoriadis and his writings that I followed his class for twelve years. Among contemporary philosophers, Castoriadis, with Isaiah Berlin and Paul Ricoeur, has had the biggest influence on my political thought. I introduced my father to Castoriadis during one of his last visits to Paris and we decided to translate some of his writings into Persian. Unfortunately my father's illness prevented this. My interest in social networks pushed me to suggest to a few of Castoriadis's friends that we start a radical philosophical group, to be called Agora International, centered on his work and thoughts. The group is still going, now run by his American translator. Without a doubt, Castoriadis had one of the great encyclopedic minds of the twentieth century and he coloured the central ideas and themes of his time. His brilliant and witty thoughts on the meaning of the Western tradition and its philosophic and political premises will long remain crucial for the understanding of our world.

My affinity for Castoriadis as a person and for his work greatly affected my ideas about democratic life in Iran. I thought of politics not as the activities or platforms of political parties but as an explicit, coherent activity that instills and develops democracy. I became more and more interested in the concept of democratic agency and the critique of totalitarian states. My readings of Hannah Arendt during the first year of the Iranian Revolution and my interest in the works of Claude Lefort and Paul Ricoeur helped me to develop contact with the literary journal *Esprit*. Olivier Mongin, its editor, welcomed me and invited me to the Tuesday gatherings of the journal. *Esprit* was more than a simple journal. It was a gathering place for writers, publishers, and social activists. Through *Esprit* I met many Eastern European and Latin American dissidents, several of whom shared my political views. Three of them became my close friends: the Czech poet Jan Vladislav, who was a good friend of Václav Havel; Alex Smolar, a Pole who worked with Solidarnosc; and the Romanian writer Bujor Nedelcovici.

In addition to holding Tuesday meetings where books and events were discussed, *Esprit* sponsored evening lectures. Early in 1988, Mongin asked me to give a lecture on Isaiah Berlin's book *The Four Essays on Liberty*, which had been newly translated into French. My lecture was well-received, and Mongin asked me to pursue my ideas in more depth and do an interview with Berlin. After a short telephone conversation with Sir Isaiah and a rapid exchange of letters, I met with him on June 6, 1988. On my return to Paris, a French editor asked me to continue the interviews and make a book out of them. We met again in London a few months later and my book *Conversations with Isaiah Berlin* was published in January 1991.

It is difficult for me to describe Berlin in a few words. For those of us who were lucky enough to know him personally, he was what Arthur Schlesinger called "a beacon of wisdom and humanity in the most terrible century in western history." He had a serene, humorous, joyous, and secular personality. But I am sure that Berlin himself would have preferred to be remembered as what eighteenth-century philosophers called an "animateur d'idées." His commitment to clarity went hand in hand with what he called "an unavoidable effort at *Einfuhlung* [empathy], however precarious and difficult and uncertain." His task as he saw it was to contribute to the history of thought by displaying, clarifying, and criticizing the master ideas that underpin Western civilization. This task required the rare gift of understanding historical events and figures in all their variety. Berlin's portraits of thinkers, politicians, and artists did not analyze their works but presented them from the inside. His contact with his subjects is usually direct and full of psychological sensitivity; Berlin never conceals these thinkers beneath a surface of prosaic exposition. Nor does he ever try to minimize the enigmatic quality of the writers. On the contrary, he shows himself to be acutely attentive to the visionary traits that informed the thinking of such men as Giambattista Vico, Johann Gottfried von Herder, Alexander Herzen, Johann Georg Hamann, and Joseph de Maistre. Such perspicacity is rarely found among philosophers and historians of ideas. Berlin has the exceptional ability to reveal to readers the concepts and categories that inspired these thinkers, while also depicting the hope, fear, excitement, and disturbances that surrounded the development of these ideas.

It is difficult to regard Berlin as an architectonic philosopher or to reduce his writings to a systematic statement. Yet, while his work ranges across many disciplines and embraces a great many concepts and ideas, there is a principal leitmotif behind his concerns and convictions. For Berlin, the history of ideas is not a way to analyze the belief systems of the past or portray progress from one idea to another; rather it is the art of understanding people's relationships to each other and to their institutions. Berlin's anti-teleological approach to history—an absence of belief in a purposeful development toward an end—and his advocacy of pluralism are perfectly consistent with his comprehensive perspective on ideas and his experience of liberal humanism as a Russian Jew living and flourishing in England. His commitment to pluralism and to moral humanism was born out of his experience of violence during the Russian Revolution and was forged in the shadow of his Kantian respect for the individual as "the sole source of morality." His defence of Herzen's "sense of reality" and Herder's concept of *Einfuhlung* made him an anti-utopian with an intuitive appreciation of the plurality of human experiences. He was vehemently against the shaping of human society according to any blueprint. His writings provide ample evidence that dialogue among different cultures and religious traditions remains valid and valuable not only because of the multiplicity of values that are influenced by this discourse but also because it enables us to avoid repeating historic evils.

Like many other intellectuals I have met or worked with, Berlin had a great impact on my thinking. He was a generous and gentle human being with an encyclopedic knowledge. I could listen to him for days and weeks and months and years. He spoke rapidly but clearly in a wonderful Oxford accent and had the reputation of being one of the fastest talkers in Oxford. His lack of religious belief, combined with his Jewish identity and his commitment to liberalism, made him a fervent opponent of all forms of monism and political and religious extremism.

What I learned from Berlin was, as he says, that "[t]he goal of philosophy is always the same, to assist men to understand themselves and thus operate in the open, and not wildly, in the dark."

Over the years I have learned that there is little point in talking and writing about philosophy without reflecting on the nature of philosophy itself. The function of the civic philosopher, a person who watches and thinks about the inhumanities and injustices of the world (most of the time in the name of philosophy), should be maintained, even if the concept has lost much of its political strength. The philosopher cannot be replaced by the tenure-track academic, even if the temper of the time suggests it. Philosophers still have a great deal to contribute to the democratization of democracy. They will be useful to human societies as long as we continue to believe that philosophy is not a futile quest. Today, the civic task of philosophy lies in the struggle between critical thinking and fanaticism. Whatever the price that we philosophers will pay for our empty hands in the battle against tyranny, we can still hope for the victory of inclusive, democratic thought. It was philosophy that gave me hope in prison. Let us not forget that it is the sum of all forms of critical thinking, which, in the course of human civilization, have enabled people to be less obedient and oppressed.

11

AS HIGHLY VALUED AS PHILOSOPHY IS BY THOSE who practise it, sceptics continue to question its usefulness in our daily lives. Socrates is quoted in Plato's *Phaedo* as saying, on the night before he died, that philosophy is practice for death and dying, which have to be confronted by everyone. And yet are we all capable of dealing with death as he did? Are we ever truly prepared to confront death? Throughout human history, from the time we became conscious of ourselves as thinking beings, we have either thrown ourselves impulsively into death or hesitated and pondered, fearing what there may be, or worse, may *not* be, after it overcomes us. Many of us have asked the same question as Hamlet in his famous soliloquy when he wonders "what dreams may come." Some of us invent pleasant or fearsome fantasies about our afterlife, others resign themselves to the likely possibility that beyond death there is nothing at all. Yet if we accept this second possibility, then a maddening question arises: What meaning can life have if it suddenly ends, wiping away every memory, every trace of our knowledge, our wisdom?

Perhaps no writer has faced this question as boldly as Schopenhauer when he asks, "How can one believe that when a human being *dies* a thing in itself has come *to nothing*?" Clearly, death ends our life, but it does not end the memory of our existence. And what about the death of others, of loved ones especially? Though they are taken from us and we can never again feel their presence, something of them stays with us. Whoever does not acknowledge this must hold that life is no more than a nightmare and death is a sweet awakening from it. We can say that our business is not with death, but with what comes before and after death. The absurd reality of death has its roots in our need to exist simply for ourselves; all attempts to prove our existence stem from our need to ignore that we are tiny, transient beings of no importance in the immensity of the universe.

When my father died after a nine-month struggle with cancer, I was not quite sure what was happening. I had tearfully expected his death all through those nine months, and when death stepped forward I took it to be an end to his suffering. But however understood, death always brings the immense pain of loss. It is on these occasions that we come closer to the essence of life as pure accident. This was on my mind when I learned from two of my father's friends that he had stopped breathing on the morning of June 20, 1991. My father was not afraid of death. His last days were as serene and peaceful as if he had courteously signed a contract with death. And yet my father never accepted life as a blessing. That is why he was interested in Manichaeism, the meditative religion that views human history as the struggle of goodness and light versus evil and darkness. Although he disliked dogmatic religions, he never called himself an atheist. There was always a dualism in my father that made him doubt the material as much as the immaterial. His acceptance of death and his desire not to be remembered in no way resemble his unforgotten memory among his students. But the simple and non-sophisticated tomb that is easily found in our family plot at Tehran cemetery is the proof of the truth that he sacrificed his life for others rather than accumulating money and fame for himself.

My father's death changed everything for my mother. She found herself in a difficult financial situation and for more than ten years she and my grandmother survived by selling the master paintings that hung on the walls of our house. She was harassed daily by real estate agents and various scoundrels who wanted to take advantage of a middle-aged widow and an old woman living in a three thousand square metre house. By the time I returned to Iran in 1992, the situation had made my mother very bitter and doubtful about the character of her fellow Iranians. As my father had predicted, my relationship with my mother became more difficult. Her courage and resilience in keeping her life together without asking for my help made me ashamed, but there was nothing I could do about it—not for the time being, and maybe never. I wished I could do better, but I was preoccupied. I was facing relentless pressure from the Iranian government and felt that I was in the grip of evil. My background as a Western-educated, intellectual Iranian was anathema to the government, and my work in France and my associations with thinkers around the world placed me in constant danger.

What I have tried to do all these years is to look hard into the darkness of Iranian society and see a little light. Sometimes we need to look directly at despair and defy it. It is in the nature of tyrannies to make the difference between right and wrong disappear, so for me the whole structure of Iranian political reality was suspect. It told me that if God has any influence in the world, that influence cannot always be benevolent. The Revolution showed me and my contemporaries that we were a lost generation. Everything I tried to do left the sword of Damocles hanging over my head. I had to live my life like a bullfighter.

It is in the challenge of death that, as Schopenhauer puts it, we return to where we came from. Our short lives are, after all, only tiny instants in the progress of eternity. With my father's death, I realized that life is an accident. Even if I live a long life, it is still certain that I will die in the end, but I cannot know how or when I will die. Acceptance of death makes the fact of dying more bearable. However strange this might sound, the fear of our own death is diminished when we experience the death of others.

The second death I experienced was my grandmother's, which happened fifteen years after the passing of my father. I remember my grandmother, Massomeh, as a loving soul who never ran out of kisses for me. From a traditional background, she was wed at the age of sixteen to a modernized man, my grandfather, in the early 1930s. The transition from a traditional background to the modernist lifestyle dictated by my grandfather made her suffer deeply. In the 1930s, modernist ideas had begun to surface in Iran, not only in urban planning and education but also in the dress code. The new dress code unveiled many Iranian women, but in the long run it allowed them to choose to wear the veil or to wear modern clothing. I still remember photos of my grandmother wearing a fur coat and a hat and driving a Gaz Volga car. However, despite having all the luxuries of the modern world, my grandmother did not easily adapt to her new life. When I was a child, she lived with us in a house that was also shared with my Uncle Behrouz. We had a Persian garden with a small pool only two feet deep, which I enjoyed swimming in. I remember once pushing our maid, Naneh Sakineh, into this pool while she was making her *wudu* (ablution). The poor woman didn't know how to swim and was so terrified she would drown that she forgot that the pool was shallow. She was finally saved by my uncle.

When I was a child I was scared of thunderstorms. If there was one clap of thunder, I would hide underneath my bed. Nothing would reassure me except my grandmother getting a bottle of blue potion and sprinkling some of it in the pool. She must have thought that the potion, which turned the water blue, was better than nothing to calm me down, and it must have worked because I was never struck by lightning.

My Uncle Behrouz, who was eighteen when I was born, was a close member of the family. He was tall and handsome, with greyish eyes and a good knowledge of English. He was a self-made man who never had a proper university education but still became a poet and a painter. He was also an alpinist and once saved the lives of several hikers who were lost on Mount Damavand, just north of Tehran. He later became the director of the Iranian Broadcasting Company in Delhi and after the Revolution left Iran for Turkey. He is now living in Istanbul and leads a tranquil life as a poet with his second Turkish wife, Ruki, who teaches law at Marmara University.

My three aunts, Ziashraf, Khadij, and Ghamar, who were from my grandfather's first marriage, were older than my grandmother (their stepmother) and because of this age difference they patronized her. My grandfather, Agha Zia, was the son of Sheikh Fazlollah Nouri, a prominent Muslim cleric in Iran at the turn of the twentieth century. An ultra-conservative, Sheikh Nouri opposed secularism and constitutionalism and in 1906 declared a fatwa against the new constitutional government, announcing that all members of the new parliament and government were pagans and atheists. For this, he was arrested, found guilty of treason, and hanged by the constitutionalists on July 31, 1909. A crowd of several thousand gathered before sunrise to watch him being hanged. It is said that his last words were, "Either this system must go or Islam will perish." For years his photo hung in our living room. I was told as a child that the photo had been taken by a constitutionalist who had been sent to assassinate Nouri. My mother had great respect for her grandfather. She was among those who, long before the Revolution of 1979, rightly thought of my great-grandfather as a Shiite scholar and not necessarily an ideologue. But the Iranian Revolution changed everything in our lives, including the perception we had of our own past. There were many myths about Nouri and his execution. It was said that one of his sons was a fervent constitutionalist who, when Nouri was executed, sang revolutionary songs and distributed sweets among the spectators. This man's son was Nourredin Kianouri, the General Secretary of the Iranian Communist Party. So you could say that political adventurism, both on the right and the left, runs in our family.

I was never immune to Iranian politics and it finally transformed my life, making my fate unpredictable. But there are powers in humans that transcend history and defeat destiny. Life realizes our dreams as it confronts us with our nightmares. One of my nightmares is to lose my mother. The day I learned that she had been hospitalized because of the stress my imprisonment was causing her, I cried. I have never loved any person as much as my mother. All through my life, she has been my truest friend. She has a big personality, which I sometimes find difficult, but I have always been able to lean on her during severe trials and dark clouds of doubt. I am what I am in life because of the moral and intellectual education I received from her. She has always understood what I have to say and what I do not say. We have our differences, more than I did with my father, but at the end what remains is love and respect. My mother is a playwright to her core. However, this is not all that she is, and not all that she wanted to be.

After my father's death my mother found a new, all-important mission for her life. She started helping runaway girls in Tehran and around the capital, visiting them in correctional facilities and finding sponsors among her friends for their studies and other matters. Social work was the well from which she drank and refreshed herself. Her commitment to it verged on the religious. She never wandered off, got distracted, or flinched from the goals she set herself. Once she had made her decision, she followed it through with a fierce will and a deep sense of purpose. She continued writing and translating; she translated several of my books from English and French into Persian. More than any other woman in my life, my mother is interested in my writings. She has a collection of my books in all languages and still reads the articles I've written for Persian, English-language, or French journals.

After I returned to Tehran in 1992, it didn't take me long to discover that I was always welcome to talk with her about books, art, and politics. No matter how distracted or tired she was, if I made a literary observation, her eyes would snap into focus. It was only as a student at the Sorbonne that I started reading her plays and comparative work on myths, religions, and literature. It is a pity that it took me so long to appreciate the originality and profundity of her writings. Later on, I realized how much I had learned from my mother. Her commitment to her work and her moral responsibility made a lifelong impression on me. I wish she could stay with me for a long time. I do not know if love vanquishes death, but I do know that death is not victorious as long as we keep in us the memory of others.

Now I was sitting in that tiny cell thinking of death. What is death? Is death when life ends or is it when life loses all its meaning because it was not lived as it might have been? The paradox is that death should not be thought of in terms of death but in terms of a life. When we face death, death ends and we can come into our own life. I only wish that my death is a response to my own life, as in Rilke's prayer: "O Lord, grant to each his own death." I don't want to die for others. Dying for others is a vain and futile thing to do. One has to live with others; this is the true responsibility in life. It is this responsibility that makes us responsive to life in general. It requires that I respond to life around me and makes me responsible for life. I do not say this because I want to be in good conscience when I find a resting place. Goodness does not have the last word when we are prisoners of evil. It is only when one is faced with nothingness that the self is exposed to evil. It is as though, in the silence of confinement, evil has concealed a lie. Prison is a place that forces human beings to despise themselves. But then, no matter how brutal the confinement may actually be, it mysteriously puts forward hope. Man is not what he thinks he is: he is what he hopes. Hope leaves a trace of itself in the ambiguous pain of living in solitary. Here I see the *not-yet* of death. Here, I see the impossibility of dying. The hope is always yet to come. With hope, I can damn anything, even the not-yet of death. After all, hope is a revolt against the worst of our fate.

12

THE 1,071ST APHORISM I WROTE IN PRISON SAYS, "A philosopher puts himself in danger because of his thoughts; for his philosophy is like a tightrope on which he walks, with the world threatening deep below." My ideas had landed me in prison. And I had come to the conclusion that, to get out, I would have to convince my captors that I regretted having those thoughts. As painful as it was for me to contemplate betraying my ideals in any way, no other option remained. The spectre of Bukharin continued to haunt me. I remembered reading about the eerie laughter of the public at Bukharin's trial on February 23, 1937, and Bukharin's response: "It's easy for you to talk about me. What will you lose, after all? Look, if I am a saboteur, a son of a bitch, then why spare me? I make no claims to anything. I am just describing what's on my mind, what I am going through. If this in any way entails any political damage, however minute, then, no question about it, I'll do whatever you say. (Laughter.) Why are you laughing? There is absolutely nothing funny about any of this ..." It's always easy to accuse people of betraying their ideals when history betrays itself by devouring its own children. Perhaps I was not betraying my ideals but simply betraying history by turning my back on it. This kind of betrayal is possible only if you still have dignity in life. We are always confronted by betrayal because, in the end—whether we have betrayed our selves or not—there is part of us that knows there's absolutely no such thing as a betrayal. Deep down, it is a suspicion of mistrust between one's inner voice and oneself.

In those weeks, an unexpected series of events began, allowing me to chip away at the walls that confined me in order to secure my freedom. In the early hours of the morning, after I'd finished exercising and had started reading, I heard a banging on the cell door. The slot then opened and a voice told me to prepare for a visit. A minute later, Hajj Ali and Hajj Saeed came in and, after going through the usual routine, took me into the corridor. But, this time, instead of giving me a shave and change of clothes and blindfolding me, they led me straight outside, away from Section 209 and into the prison garden. The few trees, patches of grass, scattered wildflowers, and a bench seemed utterly misplaced in this grim setting, but

their reminder of the outside world immediately com-
forted me. It reassured me to see that such things still
existed. But I had no idea why I was there. Hajj Ali and
Hajj Saeed stood next to me, saying nothing and gazing
about impatiently. A few uniformed soldiers passed by. As
I looked around, I noticed the prison hospital. I deduced
that the garden was for the use of doctors and patients,
offering them a brief respite from the bleak activities of
each day. Later I learned that torture victims and those
on hunger strikes were taken to this hospital.

Most people do not know that the doctors at Evin
Prison are anything but doctors. They do not work to save
lives but to keep prisoners alive so that the interrogations
and torture can continue. They are neither believers nor
people who uphold their oath to heal people. The only
thing that matters to them is status and money. I know
for a fact that there were doctors at Evin Prison during
the Shah's time who slept easily at night despite the hun-
dreds of tortured prisoners on their conscience and who,
after the Revolution, easily changed ideological camps and
began collaborating with the Islamic regime. In nothing
do people more nearly approach evil than in betraying
their own responsibilities.

Despite my uncertainty, I tried to enjoy the moment,
breathing deeply to take in the fresh air, listening to the
birds singing, hoping my visitor would be Azin. And, a

minute later, I saw her figure emerging in the distance. To my surprise she was accompanied by her father and they were both walking toward us from the main gate. Watching her approach was like witnessing the gradual manifestation of a dream figure; a person alive every hour in my thoughts became real, in the flesh, before my eyes. My interrogators had told me so many times that I might never see her again that I had started to believe them. Now that she was here, I wanted to cry for joy. But I kept myself composed as she finally reached us. She held her hands out to me and looked me over with concern. I realized that I must look wretched.

"How are you, my dear?" I said. "How is Afarin?" I could see that in her eyes, too, there was a real sadness.

"We're both fine. Today, Afarin took her first steps," she responded softly. "You look terribly thin."

"Do I? Never mind. How is my mother? And the rest of the family?"

"Everyone is well. We're worried about you, though. Do you know when you'll be freed?"

It was a painful question for both of us, and she asked it with such feeling that the words broke something in her and tears started to roll down her cheeks. She had been so strong, but it was impossible for her to hold back her emotions any longer. Hajj Ali and Hajj Saeed, who overheard our exchange, turned away and walked off a few steps. I reached out and put a hand on her shoulder, looked into her eyes.

"I will get out of here eventually. Have hope," I said, trying to impart to her the same comfort that her visit had given me.

I learned later that she had recently met with Judge Saeed Mortazavi, the city's Prosecutor General, who had told her that it was very unlikely I would be freed. So her tears kept falling even as she handed me some pastries, even as she hugged and kissed me, even as we walked away from each other, constantly looking back and wondering how the visit could be over so quickly.

There was little time to think about what we had said, however. As soon as I was back in Section 209, I was taken to a room where a taciturn barber gave me a quick shave and a haircut. "Why now?" I kept wondering. The last time they had tidied me up like this was *before* the visit. What were they preparing me for now? When the barber finished, Hajj Ali came in with some clothes from my luggage and told me to change.

"Put these on. You have to look good for the camera."

"The camera?" I asked. "Are you planning to film me for something? I don't want to be filmed."

"Shut up and do as you're told," he yelled. He rarely let his anger flare up like this. But then he continued, "That wife of yours is creating a lot of problems for us.

And now you will do something for us to cancel out those problems. Anyhow, this is part of your interrogation and you have no say in the matter."

Now I understood the reason for his anger. Even though he wasn't willing to say it openly, and Azin had had to conceal it in front of them, the campaign to secure my release had gained a lot of momentum and pressure was mounting on the prosecutors to charge me formally. And to charge me, they required more evidence. A confession, they thought, would work best.

The makeshift way they had arranged everything was almost comical, considering their status as agents of the state. They were more like goons, henchmen in a criminal organization, than professionals serving the government. I walked the distance from my cell to the interrogation room blindfolded. Once there, they took off the blindfold but told me not to move my head in any direction. The room was like the other interrogation rooms, except that here they had replaced the usual metal chair with a brown leather chair; behind it stood a blue screen and in front of it was a table with a microphone. A single plant next to it was supposed to make the place look pleasant. One of the interrogators, who never showed me his face, was sitting on my far right so that I could not see him and he would not be on camera. Two cameramen at the other end of the table said they were ready to begin filming. Hajj Ali sat me down on the leather chair and barked out his instructions.

"You are to repeat everything we tell you in front of the camera. You may not change any of the words and you have to say it all as naturally as possible. Listen closely and memorize the words well, because we don't have all day. Most importantly, we will be standing to the side and you are *not* to look at us at any point. Keep your eyes averted, or else we will have to stop the tape and start again, and it will not turn out well for you if you keep wasting our time. On the other hand, if you comply and do exactly as you're told, there may be some hope for you after all."

They had orchestrated everything quite cleverly. They had taken me to see my wife and immediately afterward, knowing I would be excited and anxious to be released, had brought me here to force a false confession out of me. More than anything, they had used the element of surprise against me; it all happened in a whirlwind, leaving me no time to contemplate my next move. It was very effective. The image of Azin—her cheerless eyes, the tears streaming down her cheeks, her trembling lips—was freshly burnt into my consciousness. I had to do whatever I could to get out of there, to be with her and my daughter again. I was not going to be like Socrates, ready to drink the hemlock. Unlike him, I felt I had too much to lose.

"Tell me what to say," I told Hajj Ali.

I had nothing to confess. I merely repeated their words. Keeping my eyes down the entire time and reciting it all as bluntly as I could, I said that my work on nonviolence was directly tied to the interests and designs of the United States; that American agents had approached me and put me in contact with people at the National Endowment for Democracy (NED) and this had given shape to my plans and aims. None of this, of course, was true. My fellowship at NED required me to collaborate with the *Journal of Democracy*, which I did, and nothing more. But, of course, this was considered espionage, though spies rarely have time to do research and write on philosophical or political issues. At the end of my fellowship, I said, I had prepared a report comparing Iranian civil society with that of Eastern Europe at the time of the velvet revolution. I was also supposed to have been in contact with people at the Woodrow Wilson International Center for Scholars in Washington D.C., in particular the director of its Middle East program, Haleh Esfandiari—who, they told me to mention, is married to a Jew. The aim of the organization, I told the camera, was to foment unrest and eventual revolution in Iran.

This was, of course, a part of a game prepared by the security officers to delegitimize me as an intellectual and to present me as the person who had disclosed the name of Haleh Esfandiari and others during my interrogations.

However, things were not as they appeared. I was arrested because of Haleh Esfandiari, who was arrested after me. At the time I was not sure that she would be arrested, but after my liberation, despite the twenty-four-hour surveillance of the security officers I asked my mother to inform Haleh through intermediaries about the intentions of the Iranian security forces, but unfortunately we could not get in touch with her before she arrived in Iran.

"Now that I am looking back at my activities over the past few years from America to Iran," I finished with suppressed bitterness and pain, "I see that my activities have placed me in the camp of Iran's enemies rather than on the side of its national interests. And I am disappointed in myself for these things and I think that I have to rectify this in the best way possible."

To my relief, the camera was turned off at this point, and I was congratulated on having done a good job. This, Hajj Ali told me, would really help my case. With mixed feelings of satisfaction and disgust, I returned to my cell and hoped for the best. As I lost myself in the pages of Hegel's *Phenomenology of Spirit*, the cameramen took the video to get it transcribed and soon word got out that I had confessed to being a traitor and spy. The tape itself would not be released until a year later, when it was combined with forced confessions from Haleh Esfandiari and the scholar Kian Tajbakhsh, who were both held at Evin

Prison for months in 2007, and shown in a program titled "In the Name of Democracy." This short documentary, which was aired by a state-run station, depicted the three of us as agents working for foreign interests to undermine the Islamic Republic. It began by talking about Gene Sharp and his writings on nonviolence and revolution and, interspersed with interviews and discussions, made the usual claims about the United States' diabolical schemes and the mechanisms it used to achieve its aims. To this day, certain labels have stuck to me because of this propaganda. It is true that my intellectual work revolves around nonviolence and resistance, yet I have never been a civil activist or—it goes without saying—an agent of any government. One of the reasons such accusations have been thrown at me, however, is my involvement with many different thinkers, some of them known radicals.

While I lived in Iran in the 1990s, I was attacked by some collaborators of the regime for inviting foreign intellectuals to speak at conferences and seminars. Among those I invited were the scholars and writers Paul Ricoeur, V.S. Naipaul, Michael Ignatieff, Toni Negri, Richard Rorty, Jürgen Habermas, Ashis Nandy, Agnes Heller, and Adam Michnik. They were all formally invited by their own embassies; the Iranian government had no involvement except in issuing their visas. The speeches and lectures they gave created a great deal of interest among students and other young Iranians. On some occasions, as many as a thousand people came to hear them. The government and some intellectuals who worked with the establishment were embarrassed, not to say humiliated, by the great interest shown in these talks and berated me. After the video aired, I once again found myself being attacked by supporters of the regime.

THE VISITS OF European, Asian, and North American intellectuals to Iran in the 1990s had a great impact on the progress and self-confidence of Iranian civil society. They helped to reinforce the stand of intellectuals and scholars against the isolation of Iranian society and, at the same time, helped to facilitate connections to the outside world. In inviting public intellectuals to Iran, my intention was always to help enrich the public sphere. My knowledge of French culture was very useful because Iranians have long considered France to be a cultural Mecca. I was able to help many students who wanted to know more about France and French philosophy, and to make French culture more present in Iran.

When I invited Ricoeur in 1995, I suggested that he lecture in both French and English so that he would reach more people at the conference. His philosophy was not well-known in Iran but the audience was very receptive to his ideas on history and forgetfulness. I travelled with him to Isfahan, where we stayed for two nights at the Shah Abbas Hotel and saw the city's sights. Many Isfahanis like to gather on the famous Si-o-Seh bridge, and we encountered one man there who was sitting by himself and singing, which surprised Ricoeur. I told him this is what we do in Iran. In Persian, we call this *hal*, which means to be in the present. When you are singing, you are in a metaphysical present, taking time into your presence. Ricoeur found the concept fascinating. I explained that much of Iranian culture was founded in such daily activities.

The day before Ricoeur and I left Isfahan, we received a call from the hotel receptionist saying that there was a man in the lobby who wanted to meet Mr. Ricoeur. We spoke to him on the phone and learned that he was a Lazarist priest who was in charge of a large French-speaking school named Blue Star. We agreed to meet him later that day, and that afternoon we walked two blocks through the heat to the school. After we rang the doorbell, a thin old man appeared with a dog beside him and answered in French. It was the priest and he invited us in. The building was immense—much larger than we had expected. And, more surprisingly, it was completely empty. He told us that the school had closed down after the Revolution, and he was the only one left. Ricoeur and I were captivated by his story and by the very fact of his existence and the unlikely survival of the school. He showed us around, served us homemade wine, and impressed Ricoeur with his extremely dusty collection of *Esprit* magazines, which he had amassed since the 1930s. The old man explained to us that all the other priests had left but he had decided to stay because he had lived in Isfahan for a long time and wanted to die there. Ricoeur, a man of faith himself, thought the priest's self-sacrifice was noble. All in all, it was a mesmerizing and nostalgic encounter with a remnant of the old, cosmopolitan Iran.

The purpose of the lectures was to try to bring back that spirit of multiculturalism and cultural exchange. Their effect varied from one lecturer to another. Some, like Toni Negri, caused a considerable stir because their controversial stances and philosophical approaches ran counter to the simplistic, Manichean oppositions embraced by the Iranian regime. Many Iranian leftists were surprised by my friendship with Negri, and during his visit one of them approached and said that he was happy that a liberal like me had invited a radical like Negri. This alone should show that I am far from embracing one viewpoint and that I do not support one "American agenda" as the solution to Iran's problems. The sad reality, however, is that many of those who are still concerned about American imperialism are quick to point a finger at anyone who criticizes the things the United States has also spoken against.

I have been an advocate of nonviolent change in Iran, not because I want America to invade Iran and to bring with them the "gift" of democracy but because I hope for real change wrought by Iranians; because I regret the state of things in a country I love and want to defend, a country with good-hearted people who are capable of living more nobly and compassionately. I was never able to get this across to my inquisitors in prison, but I hope that my new inquisitors today can begin to recognize this fact and join with those of us who want a brighter future for Iran.

The truth is that fanatic movements in Iran have never been able to stop critical ideas from crossing its national boundaries, and by the year 2000 it was incapable of resisting the rise of a counterculture, which culminated eight years later in the Green Movement. Many Iranian intellectuals managed to establish themselves as moral and spiritual authorities during this period. This made us powerful players in the public sphere, where we entered into open debate with those known as religious reformers. During the early years of the twenty-first century I wrote many essays on this issue and openly debated scholars such as Abdolkarim Soroush, Mohsen Kadivar, and the cleric Hasan Yousefi Eshkevari. I also organized workshops and lectured during the summer student festivals at Amirkabir University of Technology. Around this time I invited Agnes Heller from Hungary and Adam Michnik and Alexander Smolar from Poland to speak. I knew Adam and Alex from the 1980s, through my collaboration with *Esprit* in Paris. I followed the news coming out of Eastern Europe very closely, especially concerning Poland, and participated in the demonstrations organized against the communist military coup d'état in Poland. Alex was a member of the *Esprit* group and I had learned a great deal from him about Eastern European intellectuals.

In 1979, many Iranians had no idea what a totalitarian state was, because most of us had not been affected by Nazism or communism. For a long time the Iranian left dismissed the claim that communism in the Soviet Union and Eastern Europe was a form of totalitarianism. This attitude reminds me of what Arendt formulates beautifully in her book *The Origins of Totalitarianism*. She says, "While the totalitarian regimes are . . . resolutely and cynically emptying the world of the only thing that makes sense . . . they impose upon it at the same time a kind of super sense which the ideologies actually always meant when they pretended to have found the key to history or the solution to the riddles of the universe." Through my readings of Arendt and Raymond Aron and my encounters with Eastern European intellectuals, I knew that the concept of totalitarianism could be useful in advancing comparative political analysis and political understanding in Iran. I agreed with Michnik, who had remarked in 1985 while defending the term totalitarianism, "There is no non-totalitarian communism. Either it is totalitarian or it ceases to be communism."

I believed and continue to believe that there is no such thing as a religious democracy: a regime is either religious or democratic. Once we started to use the word "democratic," Iranian civil society per se was no longer religious. However, my problem was that, while the rhetoric of fighting totalitarianism could mobilize the pluralist imagination, it could just as easily create a political myopia and lack of moral clarity, sometimes despite the best of pluralist intentions. Perhaps worst of all, it could replace one form of intolerance, dictated by the exaltation of religion and the cult of the past, with another form—the rejection of religion and the worship of progress. Pascal used to say, "We are usually convinced more easily by reasons we have found ourselves than by those which have occurred to others." This is true of our situation in Iran. The actors in Iranian civil society need to find their own logic and practices rather than adopting those imposed on them. But this cannot be done without intellectual maturity. Maturity is the prerequisite for pluralism in Iranian civil society. I am referring here to Kant's definition of immaturity as the inability to use your own understanding without the guidance of another. In other words, I believe that the public use of reason is the precondition for democratic life in Iran. This is why my aim has been to further critical reasoning in the public sphere. Taking this approach is living on the edge, but perhaps one cannot think differently without living on the edge.

IN MY SMALL cell, far from the sound and fury of the world, I found myself on the sharp edge of destiny. For the first time in my life, I was afraid for the future. The truth is that I was trying to save myself from my destiny. My hope for the future was a broken-winged bird. I had to keep faith with my inner voice, and I was heartened by the words of Martin Luther King Jr.: "Man is man because he is free to operate within the framework of his destiny." If I was free to will and to act within my destiny, and if being free was in my destiny, I was sure that freedom would come to me no matter what.

I passed the days walking silently in my cell. Freedom was all I wanted, but hoping for it made me desperate. Absurdity was holding me in its grip. My desire for freedom mocked absurd injustice, but absurd injustice denied my freedom. Then one day, the moment I was waiting for arrived.

"Get ready," shouted one of the guards as he opened the steel door of my cell. "Someone will take you to the Revolutionary Court." The words "Revolutionary Court" so terrified me that I was silent for a few seconds, thinking this was the end. Then I said, "Okay. I will get ready!"

An hour later a man came, blindfolded me, and took me to a car. He took off the blindfold and I found that I was sitting in the back of an official car with the guard next to me. I was handcuffed and he had a pistol on his belt. The car was heading fast toward downtown Tehran along the road that is reserved for police officers and official cars. This was my first time out of Evin Prison in three long months. I was in my prison uniform and unshaved, and people who stopped at the red light next to our car looked at me as if I were a circus animal. I imagine they thought I was a criminal, perhaps a drug dealer. People were afraid of me because they did not understand me. For them, because I was in prison uniform, I was just a prisoner. Life is full of surprises. One day you are a respected man and the next day, when you are in prison, people find an excuse not to know you or your family. Others make you into an object of sacrifice. For them, you either die as a hero or live as a traitor. This is the logic of mediocre minds. Early in life, I learned that mediocrity is the most widely distributed trait in the world. I agree with Heidegger when he defines "the pre-eminence of the mediocre" as the "darkening of the world, the flight of the gods, the destruction of the earth, the reduction of human beings to a mass, the hatred and mistrust of everything creative and free." My experience in prison convinced me that mediocrity can never be noble—not in any form, nor for any purpose whatsoever. And now I found myself in a world of mediocre men who presumed to have a claim upon me.

The driver took us near the Grand Bazaar and parked in front of the Revolutionary Court. I was taken to the first floor where I sat for an hour with my guard waiting for Saeed Mortazavi to see me. When I was escorted to his office, he was talking to his secretary and did not even notice my entrance. He looked shorter than he did in his photos and had a three-day beard and moustache. His glasses made him look even more atrocious than his nickname, "the Butcher of the Press," suggested. Like most Canadians, I knew him for his alleged role in the death of Zahra Kazemi, the Canadian-Iranian photographer who was tortured, beaten, raped, and killed after she was detained in 2003.

Mortazavi gave me a harsh look and said, "Mr. Jahanbegloo, you are accused of spying against the interests of the Islamic Republic of Iran."

"But I have never been connected with any foreign intelligence," I replied.

"Listen to me carefully," he snarled. "If you contradict me you will go on trial and face charges of communicating with a hostile government, and I can easily ask for the death penalty."

"But I am not a spy; I am a philosopher," I said.

"That doesn't interest us. What interests us is what foreign institution you are connected with," he fired back.

"None!"

"And who recognizes you as a philosopher? Americans, Canadians, the French?"

"I . . . I've taught everywhere. But I haven't done anything except serve people."

"Is that so? And why do you have Canadian citizenship? This is a proof that you are a spy."

"But many Iranians have dual nationalities," I said.

"You are not an Iranian; you are an ugly Canadian."

"But I have lived and worked in this country. I have written books in Persian."

"Your writings are of no use to us. They do not serve Islam and they do not serve Iran."

Mortazavi turned to Hajj Saeed and said, "Take him to the other room and read him all the accusations."

I was taken to the next room and Saeed showed me a sheet of paper on which there was a long list of accusations: spying, working with foreign intelligence, plotting against the security of the Iranian state, preparing a velvet revolution, collaborating with Jewish institutions, writing lies about the Holocaust, and so on.

"Sign this," he said.

"But I haven't done any of these things!" I replied, feeling disoriented.

"Look. If you don't sign, we have to start the interrogation from scratch. That means that you will stay in prison for a year or two with no contact with the outside world."

I felt that I was signing my death sentence and that it would be used against me as long as the Islamic regime remained in place in Iran. But many prisoners before me had done the same thing to save their lives and get to see their families again. I was no different. I was thinking of my daughter, Afarin. What would she think twenty years from now? Would she say that her father was a hero, a coward, or simply a man who met his destiny on the road he took to avoid it?

I was taken back to Evin. My supper was waiting for me in the room, colder than usual. The blindfold was taken off. The steel door closed behind me. That night I ate and slept with shame.

13

PRISON KILLS TIME, BUT NEVER DESTROYS HOPE. The question that is constantly on the mind of a political prisoner is not "Why am I here?" We know we are in prison for our ideas. Rather, the question that haunts us is "When will I be freed?"

My emotions were never stable in prison. With so much time on my hands, I could go from being disappointed to angry, to hopeful, to melancholic, to fearful, to rapturous, and back, all in the course of one day. Like Proust in his novel *In Search of Lost Time*, I was able to explore the most minute spaces in my past, pieces of my history buried so deep that I had assumed they were gone forever. More and more, I felt myself approaching the world of writers, never far from the realm of philosophers. The main difference, of course, is that writers voluntarily shut themselves away from the world and return to it when they need to, but I was forced into this solitary space and told myself stories just to keep my sanity.

More than anything, pain was gaining an advantage over all my other emotions and was slowly stifling me. I had already missed my daughter's first steps and, on August 12, I also missed her first birthday. It should have been a special occasion to celebrate the gift that life had given me, but I had to endure the day in my cell without even a brief phone call to her. Solitary confinement is an empty shell full of demons. It occurred to me that others might see this hell as a place where saintly heroes are forged. If that were the case, I did not want any part of it. I did not want to cheer on the false prophets who promise sufferers ascension to an empty heaven. Alas, false prophets cannot always be recognized, and the heaven predicted by them very often only opens the door to radical evil in politics. The world has not become a better place because of human suffering. If we must suffer, let us suffer without being made into heroes. There is only one way to escape suffering in this life and that is to measure it against the reality of injustice, not against the hope of salvation. Salvation lies nowhere else than in life itself. Life needs to be given a meaning, and that is exactly what a sufferer confronted with meaningless violence has to do. Struggling for one's life gives meaning to life in general.

I let my anguish nourish me. I channelled it so that it kept me energized and desperate to escape, awakening in me new abilities I did not know I possessed. Nietzsche was absolutely right when he said that suffering begets creativity, that in the face of great calamity, invention and determination take root and lift the sufferer to new heights. I threw myself into this great river of life-energy and began to weave stories to survive.

IN MID-AUGUST, after the disheartening meeting with Mortazavi, my interrogations resumed and became stricter than ever. Hajj Ali and Hajj Saeed became more forceful and insistent about extracting information from me. Now that I had signed a confession saying the accusations against me were true, they treated me like a real spy, a criminal who deserved no respect or dignity. Though they didn't beat me, they threatened and insulted me, calling me the worst names they could think of and assuring me that I would spend the rest of my days in Evin Prison. After a few days of this senseless cursing and abuse, they concluded that I had no new information to give them and took me back to see Mortazavi. This time, however, the general prosecutor refused to see me. I was left outside the closed door of his office and instead received a summary of allegations against me from Hajj Ali.

"The *aghayan* are not happy, Mr. Jahanbegloo," he told me, referring abstractly to the higher authorities who were deciding my case. "They have seen the tape and they're displeased. They think your guilt was not authentic. Your movements, for instance, were unnatural. You kept looking down at the table, sputtering out the lines like a mischievous child who's been scolded by his superiors and is merely telling them what they want to hear without any genuine remorse about what he's done. You have to give us more. Otherwise, you will not be freed."

They wanted more information to support their lies about me, but what could I give them? When they took me back to my cell I understood, finally, that anything was better than what I had said so far. They weren't buying my story. They didn't consider me to be merely a scholar; they genuinely believed I was a spy. And, having already admitted to being one, I realized I had nothing to lose by going along with their diabolical game. I would be the spy they were looking for; I would give them what they wanted. The perfect opportunity arose at the start of my next interrogation, when Hajj Ali delved into new territory.

"We have been digging through your work for the millionth time and finally came across something very interesting," he said. "You see, we're not amateurs; we've dealt with many people like you before. And we've discovered a weak point in your story that exposes your guilt. We have seen, Mr. Jahanbegloo, that with all your travels and so-called philosophical meanderings, there is one place you always return to. You make yourself out to be this cosmopolitan person who has no ties to any particular place or way of thinking, but finally we have enough evidence to show that this is simply a façade you have put on. Your contacts with America and Israel were false threads all along, and you have led us in circles very cleverly. But now that we come to the main point, we have you trapped. We know now for certain that your main collaborator, the foreign intelligence you worked for this whole time, has been France. Now, before we get to tell you how easily we can prove this, you can save us all a lot of trouble and tell us the facts yourself." He put his hand on my shoulder.

I shuddered when I felt him behind me, but I kept myself composed and stared through the gap under my blindfold at the corner where the wall met the floor. I tried to imagine how that seemingly impenetrable seam could be opened up, how with simple words I could tear away at these walls and find myself on the other side. Then it all came pouring out of me, from a place that to this day I can't identify.

"All right, I will tell you. You know already that I completed nearly all of my studies in France and spent many years there—many formative years. France has always been close to my heart. The richness of its culture and its political life have fascinated me since I was a child. But I guess that after I finished my degrees there, I began to get more involved with its government. I travelled there a lot in the 1990s. I met a lot of influential people, political thinkers especially, many of whom had been involved in France's colonial activities around the world. I don't know why I got mixed up with them. I suppose they found me, or perhaps saw in me an opportunity to exploit, a chance to find connections in Iran and achieve some . . . purposes here."

"Who were these people? What were their names?"

I really had their attention now. They had been silent and then, suddenly, Hajj Ali exploded with questions, thinking that all his suspicions were finally being confirmed by this new confession. I had to keep going, to inhabit the lie as I told it, to spontaneously create an unlikely yet convincing story. With hesitation, which I tried to mask as anxiety over revealing important names, I gave them some random French names just as they came to my mind. They were not the names of anyone I had ever met or even heard of, but names such as children make up during a word game. Later, in my cell, I realized that some unfortunate Frenchmen with those names—which I couldn't remember afterward—were now blacklisted by the Iranian government and probably subject to some intense scrutiny. But in the interrogation room, as I continued with my testimony, I could sense the viselike grip over me loosening.

"Anyhow, through those men, I was put into contact with agents of the state—or, I should say, that these agents came looking for me. One of them, Maurice B———, had been collaborating with me on various research projects for some time and was always insisting that I go to the French secret service with my findings regarding Iran. I refused, but he persisted. When he saw that I could not be swayed, he went to the secret service himself and they sent agents after me. One day, as I was about to board a plane to Tehran, they stopped me at the airport and took me to their headquarters outside Paris. They asked me why I kept travelling between Iran and France. I told them that Iran was my native country and that I had many relatives there, but they said I was lying and accused me of spying against France. Then they told me that an unknown source had testified against me, stating that I had been withholding very sensitive information that could be of use to the French government. They forced me to collaborate with them."

Silence pervaded the interrogation room as it never had before. They were so captivated by what I was telling them that it seemed they even forgot to breathe.

"How exactly? How did they convince you, and what did you do for them?" Hajj Ali eventually blurted.

"Well, they threatened me and told me I could easily be thrown in jail just for withholding information. The spying charges would be even more damaging. Even if they didn't manage to keep me in prison for a very long time, they could easily ruin my reputation as an academic and effectively end my career. It was time, they told me, to face the fact that the information I had uncovered was not merely of interest to scholars but was vital to matters of national security. If I did not disclose it to them, I would be endangering many lives and putting France's position in the world at risk."

"What information? Tell us what you told them!" Hajj Ali yelled. He was scribbling down every detail of what I said in his notepad.

"A bunch of nonsense, really. My research was about the political structure of the Islamic Republic, stating which figures have which powers and responsibilities and how this affects the nation's foreign policy and so on. One of these individuals was Mr. Rafsanjani. The French government believed he was a key figure in our international relations, thinking that he could easily create such hostility against France that it could lead to military action or some sort of attack against them. Because of Maurice B——'s testimony, they were convinced that my work on

Rafsanjani's role within the state was crucial information. I ended up revealing only well-known facts about Mr. Rafsanjani, things that every Iranian citizen knows. But to them it seemed to be some kind of revelation. Still, it was not enough and they insisted that I continue working for them. They threatened me further and told me that the only way they would reduce the pressure on me would be for me to cooperate. They said that I could keep travelling between France and Iran only if I brought further information each time I re-entered France. I was to report to their headquarters as soon as my plane landed and I had to have something new for them each time."

"What else did you reveal to them, you bastard? What have you done to put our nation at risk?"

I was astonished by how gullible they were; they bought into it all. I simply had to make sure I didn't go too far and incriminate myself in something too serious.

"Nothing, nothing else, I promise you. I'm opening up to you, finally, out of fear. I didn't divulge these details earlier only because I thought they did not matter. The things I told them were all insignificant. Like I said, I told them about Rafsanjani's role in our state affairs, and later, during the one time I actually flew back from Iran to France, I went to their headquarters and told them that Rafsanjani was planning to run for president again. They found this unbelievable, and it made them very concerned. The French are very stupid. And their agents are even more brutal than you. Unlike you," I said, using the formal *shoma*, "they did not hesitate to beat me. But a few basic facts and a bunch of lies were enough to keep them satisfied and they finally let me go. I haven't been back there since."

I just hoped that Hajj Ali wouldn't be able to discern the mockery, which was impossible to suppress, in my words. He was quiet for a while, ruminating perhaps, or triumphant that he had finally gotten what he wanted out of me.

"Good," he said finally. "Very good."

It seemed that what I had told them not only confirmed but even went beyond their suspicions. They were still excited when they dismissed me that day, and the next day they were eager to resume the interrogation. For three days in a row I told them as many things as I could think of, making sure that I reiterated the basic facts every time to keep the story plausible. I had an answer ready for all their questions. By the time it was over, my interrogators were satisfied that they had finally gotten some concrete details out of me—details that they could use to substantiate their conspiracy theory. I could sense that this whole nightmare was slowly closing in on itself, leaving them to delve farther into madness while I found my way out.

The next two weeks went by without much incident. I sat in my cell and waited while they decided my fate. I felt quite good and believed I would be freed soon, but there were constant reminders all around me that nothing was certain. Above my cell was a corridor where they kept the telephones. Every few days I could hear a woman talking and crying loudly. Her words were indistinct but there was such misery in her voice that it dragged me down and made me forget my optimism. I also heard prayers and conversations in Arabic, which I think were those of Khuzestani activists, as well as the howling of a man—whom I took to be Mousavi Khoeini—a reformist member of the parliament, who was beaten each time he was taken out of his cell. "*Nazan! Nazan!*" he would cry—don't beat me! I learned later that eventually they broke his head open against the wall.

With the violence around me escalating each day, I focused on freeing my mind and escaping my surroundings. By now, I had trained myself to think beyond the walls of my cell and lose myself in other places. Even when I was permitted on the roof of Section 209 for fresh air, I could sense freedom only by closing my eyes and picturing myself somewhere else. The roof where I was allowed to wander alone for ten minutes each week was a cage. The little enclosed space, covered completely by metal bars that cast a grid of shadows on the concrete floor and walls, reminded me of the Hitchcock movie *Suspicion*—and it created the same feeling of dread, the sensation of being a bird trapped in a cage, tormented by the closeness and inaccessibility of freedom. Here, the only thing I could do was either run around to get some exercise or simply stand there with my eyes closed, envisaging myself in India, talking with the Dalai Lama.

I decided that my actions must be worthy of my self-respect. But how could I be a good judge of my own actions? I tried to keep my dignity, but it was difficult. I had lied to my interrogators, who would use what I'd said to present me to the world as a traitor. The truth is that the whole business of Section 209 is to make sure that people leave there with an amputated soul, unable to doubt the image that they have created. But I sold no one out to buy my freedom. That was not heroism. It was simply an attempt to keep my integrity as a human being. They had my future in their hands, but I was the one who had come to the crossroads, and I was the one who had to choose between revenge and forgiveness.

Life in confinement is a constant struggle against the spirit of hatred and revenge. Hatred has nothing to do with spirituality. It is a kind of power that manages the relation between things in the absence of love and compassion. Whenever someone is humiliated and degraded as a human being, hatred and revenge will triumph. Iranians have struggled for centuries against evil men who divide and destroy us, but we never fight against the values and norms that create these evildoers. We have never stopped the wave of hatred. Those who have faced hatred and violence have not put an end to violence and hatred. They thought freedom was the best way forward on the path to justice, but the thinking of too many of them was influenced by hatred, which makes us indifferent to the suffering of others. I don't know which makes me sicker: hatred or a depraved indifference to human suffering. I am not sure about the strength of light over darkness in the world, but I am pretty certain that love can be stronger than hatred.

Finally, on August 27, I was taken to the interrogation room, where Hajj Saeed told me with evident disdain that Javier Solana—the Secretary General of the Council of the European Union at the time—had brought a "gift" for me. Mocking him, he told me that Solana, whom he depicted as arrogant, had offered a deal to the Iranian government regarding its nuclear program and had demanded my release as part of the agreement. As a result of this pressure, I would not be put on trial and negotiations with my family were under way. Azin and my mother had put up their apartments for my bail and all that was left was the paperwork. After that, he said indifferently, I would be released. This would happen by

August 30. That night, feeling excited, I cleaned up my cell by picking up all the newspapers from the floor. I dreamt about seeing my family the next day but instead I had to endure twenty-four hours of silence—probably the heaviest hours I spent there. But at last, on the next day, my cell door was opened and I was told that I had been freed.

14

"FREEDOM," WINSTON SMITH WRITES MEMORABLY in Orwell's novel *Nineteen Eighty-Four*, "is the freedom to say that two plus two make four." With my liberty now imminent, I thought how sweet it would be to be able to think this way again. But my jailers wanted to make sure I stayed disconcerted until the very end. They released me slowly, grudgingly, prolonging the process as long as they could to remind me I was still in their hands. I had to wait one more day after they promised to free me but, finally, was freed on bail on August 31, 2006. I was asked to shave and to change into the clothes I had worn to the airport. After they took me out of my cell, they blindfolded me and escorted me out of the high security section to another building. I was fingerprinted in a small, dirty room and then taken to a big hall full of men I took to be drug dealers anxiously awaiting their fates. My destiny would be different, I told myself.

My blindfold was removed for the last time, but I kept my head down and spoke to no one until finally the paperwork was finished and I was taken to a room near the main gate. Here, most of my belongings were returned to me—my credit card and passport not included—and I was directed outside. I assumed that I could just walk out of the prison. I was wrong. Instead, I was seized and shoved into a car. I couldn't help feeling an eerie sense of déjà vu. Relax, I told myself. It wouldn't make sense for them to go through all this only to keep me captive. But I was jarred—my ability to judge the actions of others was frail after so long in solitary.

As the car was driven out of the prison and onto the freeway, I looked at the man sitting beside me. It was Hajj Saeed. I hesitated to ask him where I was being taken. Was he really taking me home? He knew where I lived because he had been part of the team that had searched the apartment. When the driver finally took an exit ramp nowhere near where I lived I finally spoke up and asked where we were going.

"To a news agency," Hajj Saeed answered curtly.

"Which one? Why?"

"Be quiet for now," he replied.

Thirty minutes later we pulled up in front of an office

building and, once I saw the letters over its main door, I understood. It was the Iranian Students' News Agency, whose journalists propagated the views of the state and slandered those who were against it. I gave Hajj Saeed a questioning look, trying to be patient and waiting for him to explain what exactly we were doing here. He lowered his window and lit a cigarette, exhaling pensively, as if trying to remember his lines. A couple of minutes passed, then he threw out his unfinished cigarette.

"You are to go in there and speak to the man at the desk. Tell him who you are. He will know where to take you. Once they sit you down in the room where you are to be interviewed, you will tell them about your activities and the reasons why you were kept in captivity in Evin. You will tell them the same things you said in your confession. You will admit that you acted against national interests and therefore endangered the Islamic Republic. You will mention the nature of your contact with foreign powers and the ways in which you collaborated with them. You will show that we had good reason to keep you in prison so long. Above all, you will be honest. No lies about any harm done to you in prison—you do not have a single mark on you—and none of that crap about psychological damage or pain and suffering from being in isolation. What you were subjected to is the gentlest form of imprisonment, so do not exaggerate. Finally, you will not speak to anyone except the journalists inside the office. You must answer their questions directly and, again, according to the testimony that you gave earlier. If you fail to do any of these things, I'll be waiting here for you so I can take you right back where you came from. And believe me—I'll be only too glad to do it. Is all that clear?"

"Yes," I answered quietly. If that was all I had to do to be free, I would gladly do it, I thought. I opened the car door and stepped out into another stifling day in Tehran. I took a deep breath and immediately coughed from the heat and the pollution. All the little details swirling around in my mind prevented me from having even a second to enjoy being outside again, without blindfolds and handcuffs. I just wanted to get on with the task at hand. I walked quickly to the main entrance, feeling Hajj Saeed's eyes on the back of my head. Once inside, I saw that everything had already been arranged and that, like a puppet, I merely had to go through the motions. The man at the reception desk recognized me immediately and took me up to a brightly lit room on the second floor. I waited there until three young men and a woman came in, three with notepads and one with a tape recorder, and began questioning me.

Their questions were all predictable and in line with what Hajj Saeed had told me to expect. And so were my answers. But I told them that even though I had worked with foreigners and acted against national security, I had not done so deliberately. I had not meant to act against the nation. My case was still in the hands of Prosecutor General Mortazavi, and it was he who would decide if I had acted knowingly and if I would be formally charged with conspiracy. In the meantime, I maintained my innocence but I would admit that what I had done was regrettable. Of course, I regretted nothing and would never renounce any of my intellectual work, but I had to embellish my story to make their treatment of me justifiable. I told the young reporters that my work on civil society was meant to be purely theoretical and academic. My comparative study of Eastern European thinkers and Iranian thinkers was all simply scholarly work. It was not politically motivated. But, I told them, it had been misused. By comparing political change in Eastern Europe with reforms in Iran, I was unwittingly preparing the path for a regime change in the Islamic Republic, something that the American government very much wanted. Yet again, painfully, I had to repeat the details of my previous forced confession: how the Americans had funded my project and supported me. But I also reiterated that I was not involved in any political activities. I maintained that all my work was non-political and my main interest was in serving as a builder of intellectual bridges between different cultures. If my work was being appropriated by those with certain political interests, that was no fault of mine.

When I'd finished, I felt I had vindicated myself to a certain extent. I anticipated that I would still be rebuked and derided from many sides, but it didn't matter to me then. My friend Danny Postel has made a perceptive comparison between my situation and that of the character Tomas in Milan Kundera's novel *The Unbearable Lightness of Being*. Like Tomas, who lived in Prague during the Soviet occupation, I was compelled to admit that my writings had been hijacked and altered by those who opposed the regime and that, whether I meant to or not, I was thereby harming the nation. The difference between us was that, unlike Tomas, who refused to give in and lost his job as a result, I went along with their lies to save my career. Did this mean that I was really admitting to some guilt in the matter? Had I sold out? These questions haunted me in the months and years to come, but my final view is that I have no regrets. I could not see myself doing anything other than philosophical work. To let myself be torn away from doing what I love most—what I must do if my life is to have any meaning—and to be estranged from all my colleagues and friends would be to consign myself to slow decay and misery for the rest of my life. No, I would not let them break me. I went along with their lies; it was the only way I could continue to work and to help create an ethos of honesty and solidarity.

When the interview was over, I was told to leave through the back door to avoid journalists from other news agencies and photographers who had gathered out front. I asked if this meant that I didn't have to go back to Hajj Saeed, who was waiting in his car for the results of the interview. The young reporters looked bewildered, and I realized my question had been pointless. With one possible exception, they had no clue who Hajj Saeed was. Ecstatic, I practically flew downstairs and out of the back of the building thinking I would catch a cab and go straight home. Then I realized what a mistake that would be. I went back inside and made my way to the main entrance and to Hajj Saeed's car. It was the right decision; he already knew what I'd said during the interview. He congratulated me on a job well done and drove me home.

Azin was waiting for me at our apartment. My mother had decided not to join us, but she sent me the most beautiful flowers that I have ever seen. A garden of different flowers whose smell and colour nourished my fragile soul. The first thing I did was to kiss my one-year-old daughter. She was now walking on her own. She recognized me and gave me a big, smiley greeting when I entered a room. After a long and tearful reunion with Azin,

I told her the first thing I wanted to do was to get out of the city. I wasn't allowed to leave the country yet, I said, but we could drive north to the cottage of a friend near Shemshak as long as I informed my interrogators where we were going. They would be watching us, but I was practically free. However, I could not meet with my friends and colleagues without putting them in danger. The day after, I went to see my mother. She had lost weight and her hair was whiter than usual. I could see on her face the trace of suffering, though she had been very courageous all through my imprisonment. This is one of the miracles of love: the power of suffering for the other.

Filled with excitement, we packed a few items and left the next day, driving into the Alborz Mountains and leaving behind the misery of the past four months. On the way to Shemshak, I asked Azin to stop at a grocery shop so I could buy a soft drink for the road. In the shop a middle-age man I had met once at a friend's house recognized me. He was extremely happy to see me. He turned to the grocer and said, "You know who this man is? He is a hero. He was just freed from prison." I suppose he had followed the news on satellite television. I was deeply embarrassed, not because of this man's kind words but because I knew that I was no hero.

I needed nature. I was desensitized from having lived within concrete walls for so long, numbed to the point of feeling inanimate. I had to rediscover *being* again, to walk among trees and flowers, to let the dirt of the mountains run through my hands. We stopped many times on the way to the cottage, pulling the car over so that I could step out and breathe, taking in the smooth, hilly landscape. When we finally arrived, I collapsed on the couch and slept for several hours. I awoke to find Azin sitting beside me. We had been mostly silent till now, communicating with our eyes; but now all the words poured like water out of a broken dam.

She told me about all the support and solidarity for my cause, about the countless intellectuals and activists who had fought to get me out of prison. Among my close friends, Karim Sadjadpour and Siamak Namazi had been particularly active in organizing a campaign in my favour, and Roberto Toscano had been especially helpful, using his political influence to contact many foreign dignitaries and thinkers. A petition had been sent directly to Ahmadinejad. Azin showed me a copy, and I was spellbound by the list of signatures, which went on and on: Jürgen Habermas, Leszek Kolakowski, Umberto Eco, Charles Taylor, Ernesto Laclau, Chantal Mouffe, Slavoj Žižek, Alasdair MacIntyre, Richard Rorty, Tzvetan Todorov, Orhan Pamuk, J.M. Coetzee, Timothy Garton Ash, Shirin Ebadi, Azar Nafisi, Noam Chomsky, Martha Nussbaum, Kwame Anthony Appiah, Zygmunt Bauman, and many, many others. I could hardly believe that so many thinkers, all very influential within their fields but also very divergent in their beliefs, had come together in such a show of unity against injustice. I wept with gratitude, knowing I was forever indebted to all of them. But I was also very proud to be among them, for in the end it is our common cause that matters.

Being away from the city gave me an opportunity to contact Roberto Toscano and his wife, Francesca. We were not able to see each other until March 2007, after I had arrived in India and organized a conference on interculturality. Meeting with Roberto was a way to reset the clock and continue our friendship. I will never forget his intellectual courage and moral strength in the fight for my cause.

We returned to Tehran after a few days, back to my "normal life," which was not normal at all. I was not able to see my friends and colleagues and my situation was worse than it had been before I was imprisoned. Mr. Khoshnevis, the director of the Cultural Research Bureau, asked me to leave and sent back all my belongings. I had worked there for three years but now had to leave all my intellectual and civic efforts behind. For almost two months I lived under surveillance in Tehran. Azin and I were obliged to meet weekly with security officers, who wanted to make sure that I was not going to meet with any foreign diplomats or give interviews to foreign journalists. I was offered the job of directing an institute in Tehran, which I refused. We were forbidden to go to the United States or Canada, but they did consider the possibility of our returning to India, where my colleagues were impatiently awaiting my return. They told me I would have to meet regularly with a person who worked at the House of Iran in Delhi and report all my contacts with foreign journalists and diplomats to him. I never met this person after I went back to Delhi, for the good reason that I never approached him.

The days after being freed were difficult. It was impossible to continue my previous social life. I felt alienated and feared that I had lost a part of myself that I could never recover. I did not call any of my friends, as I did not want to put them in danger. I met only the people who had stayed in touch with Azin and who had helped us directly. The director of the House of Artists, Behrouz Gharibpour, who, two years before my imprisonment, had invited me to teach a series of classes on Hegel's *Phenomenology*, had had the extraordinary courage to confront the accusations against me and to put his own situation in danger. At Azin's suggestion, I visited Mehdi Karroubi, the reformist cleric who had shown some sympathy for my cause. He expressed his joy that I was out of prison but then advised me not to act against the interests of the Islamic Republic. I explained that I took my work as a philosopher seriously and, for me, this meant no collaboration with the theocratic regime but, rather, that I had to resist all forms of dogmatic and anti-democratic thinking.

Then, on a sunny day in late October 2006, my Iranian passport was returned to me and less than a week later we left for Delhi. At four o'clock in the morning, at Indira Gandhi International Airport, we were received with flowers by my Indian friends Ashis Nandy and Suresh Sharma. Finally, the danger we were in was behind us, but my nightmares followed me to India. Every night I was back in my prison cell, back to the silence and the muted screams, the dirty walls, concrete, coldness, and endless uncertainty. I relived my arrest at the airport and was arrested in countless other places, harassed by face-less men with quick, powerful hands. I would wake up drenched in sweat and scared until Azin's presence by my side reassured me that it was over now. In India, reality slowly returned, as the objects and people around me resumed their rightful places in my inner world.

Seeing the Dalai Lama again was especially helpful to my recovery. In a world governed by the evils of ignorance and violence, the moral voices of people such as the Dalai Lama and Nelson Mandela have the power to restore the ability to love. I was lucky enough to have met the Dalai Lama earlier, in April 2006. We'd talked about the nature of nonviolence in today's world, and the interview had been published in an Iranian reformist newspaper while I was in prison by journalists who had risked a great deal to show their solidarity with my cause. I had been following the Dalai Lama's path and his writings for a long time and our move back to India gave me the opportunity to go to Dharamsala in the foothills of the Himalayas to have an audience with him. My wife and I, accompanied by Afarin and Didi, her nanny, hired a car to get there, driving through Punjab. On our way, we visited the Golden Temple in Amritsar, the spiritual centre for Sikhs. Once we arrived in Dharamsala, we prepared ourselves for the audience with His Holiness.

I had purchased a khata (a traditional Tibetan scarf) and a Persian carved wooden box to offer him as a sign of our respect. Khatas are usually offered to religious images, such as statues of the Buddha, but it is traditional to present the Dalai Lama with a white one. On the day of the audience, we arrived early at his residence in the suburb of McLeod Ganj. After completing the security procedures, we waited in a small room next to the audience hall. After His Holiness finished with his previous meeting, he stood as usual at the threshold to welcome us. I presented him with the box and the khata and he blessed me and my wife. Azin had brought a video camera and started filming the meeting. He invited me to sit next to him, on a big sofa, while some of his advisors and assistants sat at the other side of the room. The Dalai Lama was very curious about Iran and Islam and he started asking me questions about how Muslims could act nonviolently and in dialogue with other faiths. He was interested to learn that I was a Gandhian as he has written on Gandhi. All through our conversation, he kept smiling while giving all my questions serious answers.

The intensity of the moment is impossible to describe. The Dalai Lama's personality is unlike that of anyone I have ever met. He is as pure and innocent as a child, but as confident as a mountain standing alone. Most Tibetans and many non-Tibetans think of him as a soul who has embraced the highest levels of understanding and enlightenment. I found in him the best of human compassion, wisdom, and humility. He has said, "With the realization of one's own potential and self-confidence in one's ability, one can build a better world. According to my own experience, self-confidence is very important. That sort of confidence is not a blind one; it is an awareness of one's own potential. On that basis, human beings can transform themselves by increasing the good qualities and reducing the negative qualities." What I learned from the Dalai Lama is that the path to peace and nonviolence lies in our choices and evolution. Humankind has to escape violence, which can be done only through practicing nonviolence; this, in turn, is possible only if humanity learns to transform itself. Nonviolence, like violence, begins in our minds.

He left me with a present, a dharma wheel that I cherish to this day, and words of wisdom to keep me strong and relentless in my drive to do something good in the world.

We stayed in India until the end of 2007, travelling extensively throughout the world for conferences and speaking engagements. After that, we lived in Budapest for four months, thanks to Yehuda Elkana, former director of the Central European University, who invited me to work at the university. This allowed me to resume my scholarly work and get back on my feet academically. During our stay, we visited many European capitals, including Paris, Rome, Madrid, Warsaw, and Vienna, where my friends celebrated my freedom and asked me to give lectures at various academic and political institutions. My friends at *Esprit* in Paris, the Kreisky Forum in Vienna, Adam Michnik in Poland, Agnes Heller in Hungary, my Catalan friends and publishers, Montse and Toni, in Barcelona, and the Italian friends of the Reset group, Giancarlo Bosetti and Nina zu Fürstenberg, were especially helpful to us. I spent the summer of 2007 travelling, lecturing, and also working with Roberto Toscano on a book entitled *Beyond Violence*. My meeting with the Dalai Lama had cemented my resolve to work on the subject of nonviolence.

My imprisonment had made me think profoundly about the reasons for violence in Iran, but also more generally about what the nonviolent mechanisms of taming violence could be. A peace that is constructed with violence excludes democracy. In the words Tacitus put in the mouth of a Gaelic chieftain on the eve of battle: "They make a desert and call it peace." Peace can only be produced in common; it cannot be fought for with violence. There is no way we can prepare for peace and democracy by preparing for war. Politics can keep us out of war, but what is needed for the consolidation of democratic institutions is a lasting peace. After all, democracy is made by humans and its fate is related to the human condition. Although we can never be certain about the positive result of our actions, it is possible to strive for democracy, because it is possible to remain true to the ethical. Remaining true to the ethical; this is what I learned from 125 days of confinement in Evin Prison.

THESE DAYS, WITH my prison ordeal long behind me, I am often asked if I remain bitter about what happened to me in Iran, if I feel disconnected from my native culture or my compatriots. I hope that in writing these pages, I have shown that my answer is a resounding no. To remain bitter, to be unwilling to forgive, is to poison oneself slowly with hatred, and to detach oneself from one's culture is simply impossible. When I look back at my jail experience I ask myself the question: what is a jail? And the answer is: It's just a building. That's all it is. It's only bricks and steel. We are the ones who give it meaning with our fear. Without our fear, jail has no power. Memories linger in us; they visit us each day to remind us of the story of our lives, of who we used to be and where we came from. They strengthen us by showing us what we have lost and how we can make the days ahead better. And so I don't reproach my home country because of what has happened to me there; I merely look ahead, trying to work with others to figure out what sort of change we are capable of and what we want for the future of Iran.

Many Iranians reject the ideas of forgiveness and non-violence. According to them, someone who has suffered cannot and should not forgive, and only those who have not suffered enough can forgive. This is an argument with no foundation. There is no thermometer that can measure degrees of suffering. The belief that wrongs cannot be remedied means that there is no reason to avoid repeating them. I believe my responsibility to the other is not lived primordially as being accused or accusing, but as an act of forgiveness. What is so special about forgiveness is that it represents an end to the cycle of crime and violence, in contrast to vengeance and hatred. I've never felt hatred or wished for vengeance against anyone, not even my jailers and interrogators. I feel no hatred for them, but I do feel disgust. I am not a religious man and I do not consider human cruelty to be a sin but rather the *summum malum*, the most evil of all evils. Horror and disgust at human barbarity fills my heart each time I hear of someone committing an atrocity against another without remorse.

In Iran, the tragedy is not only that there are people who deny their involvement in cruel activities but, worse, that there are those who justify murder and torture by pointing to the atrocities committed by their victims. It is absurd to blame others for their crimes and then commit your own in the name of justice and retribution. As George Orwell says, "Revenge is an act which you want to commit when you are powerless and because you are powerless: as soon as the sense of impotence is removed, the desire evaporates also." In other words, as history shows us, our tragic sadness over past cruelties committed in the name of God, history, and freedom is permanently mingled with a perpetual fear that a new tragedy will fall on our human family. However, there are always new hopes and new dreams in a young society like Iran's today. For me, one of these hopes is the possibility of a future Iran that can and will tame its historical violence. When we talk about nonviolence and the potential for nonviolent resistance in Iran, it goes beyond the struggle for democracy. We have two political struggles going on: one is the struggle for democracy and the other is a struggle for a nonviolent negotiation. We need to integrate the two concepts in one strategy. It is a big challenge for most of us. Nonviolence is the best means to achieve social change and political transformation, but it is not a short-term solution; it is a moral high ground that we need, and of course it is going to be a difficult choice. Nonviolence is a commitment to a life principle, not a shirt we can take off and put on again. But violence is not a function of fate, because it can fail and it usually does. I think the time is ripe to talk about the process of reconciliation and forgiveness by turning past violent wrongs into future nonviolent rights.

I WISH I could end by saying that my life has seen my dreams made flesh. However, my life has been far from perfect, because I am imperfect and because no human can live a perfect life. Some wisdom is required in order to be able to filter the inessential from the essential in life. And that can only be done by nurturing life, because the wisdom of life is in life itself. I wish I had been born a century earlier, not because there would have been less prejudice and intolerance but because people had more time to become aware of each others' mediocrities and learn to overcome them. Being influenced by the same banalities is not necessarily sharing the same values. We need to create new values in a world that has forgotten where to put the truth. This is the task of philosophy today. Philosophy, as Picasso used to say about painting, is an instrument of subversion.

Thomas Carlyle believed that a hero is a person who flourishes in the fullest sense in a world filled with contradictions. Our contemporary world has produced many contradictions, but few heroes. The heroic involves excellence in daily life, and a life of excellence needs a lucidity and maturity that we cannot find in a life without thought. By that I mean looking in action at what action cannot offer, reflecting on everything, including one's death. Life as memory arrests death. But it becomes an echo in eternity that cannot be denied. Humility must always be the result of a meaningful life. After all, without humility, it would be difficult to look back at one's life and proclaim that it has been lived to the fullest possible.

The Czech philosopher Jan Patocka has written, "A life not willing to sacrifice itself to what makes it meaningful is not worth living." For me, no life is as meaningful as a life of thought that faces destiny and comes into its own. In other words, life is a task, not a given. It is the unfolding result of always striving to do things in a spirit of excellence. In the eyes of history, it is not who I was, where I lived, and how long I lived that will be important. It is the nature of my actions that will really matter, whether I made the most of my life. And about this, time will say nothing. Time will say nothing about life. It says only that we existed. And one life is not enough time to understand the meaning of one's life.

15

AFTER A YEAR IN DELHI, WHERE I HELD THE RAJNI
Kothari Chair in Democracy at the Centre for the Study
of Developing Societies (CSDS), we moved back to Canada so that I could resume teaching at the University of
Toronto. By an irony of destiny, life was bringing me back
to the same university where I had taught for three years,
starting in 1999, and the same city where I had gotten
Canadian citizenship. I was eager to rejoin old friends and
colleagues, who had been very active in bringing me back
to Toronto. We arrived in Toronto on January 3, 2008, to
a fresh but snowy start on the year and on life. Mohamad
Tavakoli-Targhi, an Iranian professor at the University
of Toronto who had been active in working for my liberation, was waiting for us at the airport. I accompanied
my wife and daughter through the immigration process.
The young immigration officer hardly glanced at us, being

so accustomed to the daily arrival of landed immigrants. Tavakoli had reserved a big car in order to help us with our luggage. It had been snowing all day and the streets were white with several inches of snow. We headed to a furnished apartment in downtown Toronto, which we had rented with the help of the Centre for Ethics at the University of Toronto. The small apartment was owned by a Mr. Davis, who spent half of the year in Florida, and was decorated with many little porcelain and glass objects. Whenever our daughter wanted to run around the apartment, we reminded her that Mr. Davis might knock on the door and punish her, a reminder that was very effective, even though Mr. Davis passed away a year later and we left his apartment for a new building near Queen's Park. The receptionist at our condo was a very kind and gentle Iranian named Parviz, who recognized me immediately. For the next six months Azin and Afarin, who spent most of their time at home, benefitted from the kindness and empathy of this man, who introduced them to the building, especially the pool facilities. Spending all day in a small apartment without any contacts with the neighbours, who, unlike many other nationalities that we met during our stays around the world, did not speak when we met them in the elevator, Canada seemed to Azin and Afarin to be a depressing place. As for me, I began to see things in a new light, criticizing everything

I saw but putting the grim past behind me and once more able to imagine a bright future.

I deeply missed the colours and tastes of India, which had been replaced by the dispassionate people and tasteless food that surrounded me in Toronto. Unlike India, which some have called the last metaphysical nation on earth that exhibits the great spiritual features of human civilization, and where I found it a pleasure to walk in the streets of Delhi and to hear and see the diversity of sacred rituals, Canada appeared to me more and more as a country with no metaphysical foundations. In saying this, I am not looking for anything sacred in Canadian society—there is no way to compare an old civilization like India with a country with a short history. But let me go back for a minute to the time I spent in India and try to compare it with what I was seeing and feeling in Canada. Canada is only one chapter in the story of my life, not its final lines. Life is time, an endurable extension of mysteries. I have to go on peeling myself like an onion, hoping that when I come to the last layer I will find what my life really is. But what should I do with all my past experiences, this fruit of life? Toss it away, as many immigrants do, and walk the world singing the praise of my host country? For years the conviction had been growing in me that the only intelligible purpose of my life was to be found in my instinctive desire for harmony and peace.

I have never practiced any religion, but I think spirituality plays an important role in the life of every human being. Each time I read about Gandhi or what he wrote, I feel as Einstein did: "Generations to come, it may well be, will scarce believe that such a man as this one ever in flesh and blood walked upon this Earth." Gandhi seems ages away, although we are separated from him by only seventy years. But he is still very relevant for our world, because he put Indian spirituality and nonviolence on our global agenda.

The years I spent in Delhi with my family were humanly revitalizing. I wish we could have continued living in India but, unfortunately, the Rajni Kothari Chair in Democracy was offered to me for only one year, although my colleagues at CSDS had generously renewed it for one additional year because of my precarious situation. While there I gave myself fully to writing and finished my books *The Spirit of India* and *India Revisited*. Both books deal directly with different aspects and characters of Indian society. While asking the question, "Who is an Indian?" I realized that there is no single answer. There is no such thing as a monolithic India. If India has any singularity, it is because it is plural. There are as many Indias as there are ways of being an Indian. India is a land of diversity, as everyone knows and everyone repeats, and therefore it is impossible to have one fixed idea of India.

However, Indians, Hindus, Muslims, Sikhs, Buddhists, or Christians know very well who they are and why they are alive. India survives precisely because of what Indians are and not because of what others would like them to be. This is captured in a famous movie, *The Party*, where Peter Sellers (as Hrundi Bakshi, an Indian actor working in Hollywood) declares solemnly, "In India we don't think who we are, we know who we are." In a country like India we need to replace Descartes' famous "cogito ergo sum" (I think, therefore I am) by "credo ergo sum" (I believe, therefore I am)—not a belief in God, but a belief in the mystery of existence. As Romain Rolland once said, "If there is one place on the face of earth where all the dreams of living men have found a home from the very earliest days when man began the dream of existence, it is India!" I don't think the gap between the glittering upper-class life in the cities and the grinding rural poverty has diminished India's dream of existence, which results from a cross-cultural dialogue that has taken place through centuries of war and peace. The spirit of India is revealed to her as a metaphysical idea. I made this spirit mine, slowly and gradually developing the invisible links that bind my existence to that of Indians like Mahatma Gandhi and Rabindranath Tagore. Reincarnation is a way for humans to improve their earlier works, and my Indian life is only one of a series of lives I have lived. All my previous selves find their voices and echoes in my Indian soul. Oh, incalculable times, when shall I be born again Indian? All my life I had looked to the future, and now the dawn of a new day was breaking on the horizon. I was moving back to Canada to live again in Toronto. This would now be my city. It belonged to me as its citizen, but I felt no sense of belonging to it as I did to Tehran, Paris, Delhi, Barcelona, and Cordoba.

The day after our arrival I went to the University of Toronto. Melissa Williams was expecting me in her office at the Centre for Ethics. She had been an important part of the network that had worked for my liberation and return to Canada. What I owe her is beyond evaluation. She had arranged for me to give a homecoming lecture at the Isabel Bader Theatre on the topic of my last book, *The Clash of Intolerances*. Nearly five hundred people attended this lecture and I was happy to see many of those I had met previously in Toronto. The president and provost of the university had also organized a lunch at Massey College in my honour. My office was ready and many people, including journalists, wanted to meet me. But for me the most important thing was to resume my teaching. I have always considered teaching as a form of gardening. I am the gardener. I plant the seed and I wait to see the bud or the flower appear in a few years. I had initiated a course on the politics of nonviolence, the first in Ontario and in Canada. I also decided to teach a graduate class on Iranian politics, finding that Canadians often spoke about Iran without knowing anything about it. For a man like me, who found himself suffering an existential crisis after imprisonment and exile, teaching was a princely encouragement and it touched me deeply, but the melancholy of immigration weighed upon my soul. There was no question of a new job or a tenure-track position and I gradually realized that the main purpose in bringing me back to Canada had been the moral mileage that many people at the University of Toronto and in the Canadian government hoped to obtain. A high-placed official at the University of Toronto had even said this to Mohamad Tavakoli, who repeated it to me. However, in the long run, it seemed that none of the specialists of Iran at the Department of Near and Middle Eastern Civilization would be happy to have me as a competitor in Iranian Studies. Despite a great deal of student interest in a course on modern Iranian politics, I was only able to teach a one-semester course on the Iranian Constitutional Revolution.

The thing I found most difficult was that many people at the University of Toronto seemed to feel that I had arrived in paradise, having been saved from a remote island surrounded by sharks. I still remember hearing an Iranian Canadian MPP at an Iranian community centre

gala declare thoughtlessly, "Canada is the greatest country on earth." This might be the case for some people,
especially Canadian MPPs who have not travelled much,
but it was certainly not the case for me. I had traded the
danger and violence of Iranian prisons for the violence
and hypocrisy of a late capitalist society. It was not a question of being part of a society with clean hands, because
I saw no hands at all, especially those that might have
helped the number of homeless people that I met every
day around Toronto. As I walked from my new dwelling
to my office, I thought to myself that a city like Toronto,
and a country like Canada, failed to make any gestures
of love and empathy. Perhaps this is because capitalism
thinks only with its brain, not with its heart, and empathy is a language of the heart. I was deeply shocked that
in most of my meetings with colleagues, journalists, and
younger Canadians, the face of love was always hidden
behind a veil of cold logic.

After the first few months of my return to Toronto, I
began to rebel against the conformism that I saw every
day. I was troubled and perplexed that there didn't seem
to be a single rebellious soul among my young students.
As well, there were many times when they considered
mediocrity to be a form of normality. At every opportunity I repeated to my Canadian students that without
nobility of spirit every society is doomed to mediocrity.

However, with one exception, Richie Nojang Khatami, who later became my assistant and my close friend, most of my students gave me the impression that centuries of human civilization had made no impression on them and that they reduced every bit of human agency to seeking grades, entering law school, and making a lot of money as a corporate lawyer. I began to feel more and more as if we were entering our twenty-fifth hour, when it is too late for any form of reason or change.

In the months that followed, I was invited to become a Scholar at Risk at Massey College and an associate fellow at Trinity College. Ironically, these invitations reminded me of the quote by Groucho Marx: "I don't want to belong to any club that will accept me as a member." Nothing had changed in my situation. I had moved from a society dominated by clerical nomenclature to an enclave of second-class snobs who were intellectually crippled by their meaningless existence in well-guarded clubs. I was especially irritated by one White woman who guarded the entrance of Massey College and who seemed to be allergic to my dark-haired Iranian colleagues, who were stopped at the door each time they wanted to have lunch with me. This was one occasion among others when I realized that what was said about Canadian multiculturalism and fair play in theory was not necessary true in practice. It is time, I thought, for a deeper exploration of the Canadian psyche and a clearer definition of what it means to be Canadian.

As the months passed and I was caught up in the cyclic drama of my new life, depression came on me like a cloud. I had to escape to Spain in the summers to feel rested and renewed. But as soon as we returned to Toronto, I had the same feeling of being in a spiritual void. It was now 2009 and every Iranian was eagerly following the post-election riots and repression inside Iran. I had started to work on my next book, *The Gandhian Moment*, for Harvard University Press and had been solicited by Palgrave to write a book on Iran and to organize a huge conference on Iranian civil society. I resumed my Saturday philosophy classes in Persian, called *Agora Philosophical Forum*, for the Iranian community in Canada. We had open weekly meetings at OISE (Ontario Institute for Studies in Education) and I began the classes with topics like freedom, ethics, modernity, and nonviolence and later turned to Hegel, Schopenhauer, Nietzsche, and Heidegger. I was excited to find a forum where I could practice philosophy in a Socratic manner, something I missed terribly in my colloquial debates with my colleagues. Though a professor in the university, I was never invited to give a lecture in the philosophy department. This reminds me of what Schopenhauer said: "In philosophy at the universities truth occupies only a secondary place and, if called upon, she must get up and make room for another attribute."

As time passed, I was besieged by what I can call the temptation of freedom. Strangely enough, I found more interest in the idea of freedom among my Iranian students in Canada, who were concerned with a non-free country like Iran, than among my Canadian colleagues, living in a free country like Canada. This was also the case with the concept of law. While my Iranian students were crying out for law as an emancipator concept, my Canadian colleagues and students looked upon it as a set of principles printed on fine paper. Most of the time, they recited the law and then leaned back and took it for granted, as if justice would be done automatically. But justice was not done. This was one of the issues I could not shy away from while living in Canada. I had a terrible feeling that every step I took was influenced by the everyday justice system, which made value decisions that affected my life and destiny.

No one remains unchanged by the experience of exile. Some lose their identity because of fear or because of flattery. Some very few are tempered by the art of questioning. I chose a third way by becoming blunt and straightforward. But I had to confront all the problems of exile. I was committed to the whole risk of living a new life. Believing in oneself was the price of survival. But problems came to me as a collection of absurdities. I was convinced, as most immigrants are in Canada, that the best way forward was to find a way to take a step toward the happiness and comfort of my child. We had a hard time finding a daycare for her and were told that people sign their kids up for daycare even before they are born. I suppose, in the same spirit, one has to sign a child up for university before the child has even learned to read and write. I wonder if such things are not a good way to lose one's faith in the sanity of Western civilization. Yet in the whole absurdity of our everyday life in Toronto, the most important issue remains for me that of diversity and dialogue. This was an untimely thought that came to me frequently. I found Toronto to be a city of diversity that pays no attention to the best way to celebrate its differences. One cannot celebrate diversities and differences without really engaging in a dialogue with them. This is what, in my opinion, differentiates Toronto from London, Paris, and Berlin. People enjoy participating in carnivals and Harbourfront Festivals, but they don't necessary learn more about Iranians, Somalis, Pakistanis, and others by eating their food and listening to their music.

I was becoming more and more aware that I lacked a Canadian identity. I started reading about Canada and listening to anyone who could show me a way to claim identity in this country. The thought of what sort of

Canadian identity would have led me to endure imprisonment for 125 days troubled me. I came up with a quote
by Northrop Frye, conceivably Canada's most celebrated
cultural theorist: "Historically, a Canadian is an American
who rejects the Revolution." This idea presents itself in a
variety of aspects. For many English-speaking conservative Canadians, it remains a label of honour. Remember
what Winston Churchill said about this country: "Canada
is the linchpin of the English-speaking world. Canada,
with those relations of friendly, affectionate intimacy
with the United States on the one hand and with her
unswerving fidelity to the British Commonwealth and
the Motherland on the other, is the link which joins
together these great branches of the human family." But
I wonder if new Canadians still believe in England in
terms of "the Motherland," a view that is more typical of a White and English-speaking Canada. Putting
aside the laws and regulations and the twenty-dollar
bill, not all Canadians really think in terms of British
royalty, although more Canadians are passionate about
Prince William and Kate Middleton than about Canadian Nobel Prize recipient Alice Munro. This would not
be the case in a country like France, which celebrated
in grandeur the fiftieth anniversary of Algerian-born
writer Albert Camus. It doesn't come as a surprise that
a French politician like Charles De Gaulle would ask,

"How can anyone govern a nation that has two hundred and forty-six different kinds of cheese?" De Gaulle was absolutely right about France and its culture, but could we say the same thing about Canada?

It is difficult to say how one is or becomes Canadian. Most nations today have a strong sense of identity but Canadians are still in pursuit of a unified identity to give a deep-rooted pattern and a spiritual meaning to their lives. In Canada, national identity is an immigrant identity. Students who share a classroom in a Canadian university or those who share an office space in a Canadian firm in Toronto or Vancouver neither have common and shared values nor participate in a shared space of identity. For my Muslim students Islam is a hard value and it comes first, but being Canadian is a soft value and always comes second. For Iranian-Canadians or Arab-Canadians who are raised in Canada, being Iranian or Arab is far more important than being a Canadian. You need a great imagination to understand how to be proud of being a Canadian—although most Canadians are—especially given the fact that First Nations were stripped of rights over their lands, effectively being treated as obstacles to resource extraction and removed, something that occurred throughout the Americas. Newcomers to this land of hope don't learn much about those who lived here before, though there has been much more coverage of this subject by the media in the last years. But discussing First Nations does not help bring dissident views to the fore. Lacking both the historical experience and the arrogance of the Americans, Canadians do not exhibit a chauvinistic sentiment of being Canadian, but at the same time there is no sense of "Canadianness" in Canada.

I had never believed that anyone who becomes part of Canada must come to the country by way of White Canadians. This has been one of the errors in the way Canadian history is presented, and yet my experience as an Iranian philosopher in Canada substantiated the idea that most of Canada is controlled by White Canadians. I was deeply perturbed by the fact that more than ninety percent of my colleagues in the Department of Political Science at the University of Toronto were White. It is true that I found it difficult to call Canada home, because home for me is a personal feeling. But I also found it difficult to have my intellectual work underestimated because I was not a White Canadian or was not a member of a well-known family in this country. I realized bitterly that education in Canada had nothing to do with knowledge but rather, despite all that is said, that money is the rule of the game. This reminded me of how the money-makers and money-seekers who rule our world have no sense of the world that they are ruining. To see this, let us go back a few years in time.

Many years ago, when I came back to Toronto after a year of post-doctoral study at Harvard University and started teaching as an adjunct professor at the University of Toronto, I was contacted by a small consulting firm. Not knowing anything about business, I was curious about what kind of help I could offer them. It turned out that I was being hired part-time as a research and development specialist, asked to help the firm develop brands and put together new concepts for workshops. My boss, a White Canadian, was a young man who had worked previously with different consultancy groups, but his knowledge of the world did not go further than the *Harvard Business Review*. His hero was Jack Welch, former CEO for General Electric. One of the workshops was prepared for a North American client, a giant multi-national firm. The Canadian CEO of this firm was a millionaire who had no knowledge of the arts or culture but presented himself as someone who appreciated French wine and opera. Once, on the occasion of a party in his honour, I was asked by my boss, who was also ignorant of anything in human culture that went beyond business and money-making, to provide our client with a good wine and an opera CD. I decided to go with a Châteauneuf-du-Pape 1998 and Puccini's *Tosca*. During the party to entertain our guest, I started talking to him about wine and opera but realized with astonishment that not only did he not know anything about wine, but he was also ignorant about very simple facts in the history of opera. The only thing that was important in his eyes was to pay a high price for bottles of French wine and to put on his tuxedo for operas at the Canadian Opera Company. This is an example of the difference between those who produce high culture and those who consume it. The former are often poor and jobless and beg for grants from the Canada Council for the Arts, while the latter flatter themselves that they know high culture because they buy books but do not read them.

This is also true for Canadian universities. While I continued to fight for a longer-term position at the University of Toronto, everyone around me talked about getting grants. This was a new phenomenon that I had not experienced in France, India, or Iran. I realized that in Canada the most respected academic is not the person who has the greatest knowledge of cultures and the achievements of civilization but the one who gets the greatest number of grants. Salaried, tenured, and pensioned, many academics find themselves chained to the wheel of a once-respected profession that grinds down their capacity for critical thinking. Narrow professional self-interests destroy their public interests. Ignoring their moral responsibilities, many academics in Canada, and in North America in general, have degraded and abandoned the idea of contributing to the public sphere and have become uncritical supporters of mass culture. This withdrawal has helped celebrities to replace academics as the most notable actors in our contemporary world. Scholars are no longer engaged in discussing values but are only interested in discussing facts. The attempt by intellectuals in academia and other professional institutions to pretend that it is politically correct and wise to dismiss the moral imperatives of the public sphere confuses ethical questions with the special needs of career-making. As a result, I found myself among people who had abdicated their authority to speak truth to power and had become incapable of carrying out their critical functions.

So what now? Where do I go from here? Where do I turn? After having lived for more than six years in Canada I have come to the conclusion that the national heroes of Canada are not intellectuals and artists but hockey players. The reason is simple: apart from hockey, the only element that shapes the collective imagination of Canadians is the cold. For me, the cold gives the sensation of endless repetition and the feeling that nothing else is going to happen. My new life in Toronto was shaped by the two real seasons of the year: winter and summer. I found Canadian winters long and tiresome, while summers in Toronto are humid and unpleasant. I used my contacts in India and Europe to travel there each year to lecture and talk to publishers. I had to get away from

the provincialism that surrounded me and from which
I was suffering terribly. I began to see Canadian multiculturalism as a very weak form of interculturalism. I
was convinced that more than anything else it was about
laws and regulations—and lines. I found it ridiculous that
everywhere in Canada we need to respect lines: a red line
at the airport, a white line in the buses, a yellow line in
Service Canada offices, as if without lines we would have
no sense of law and society. But when regulations go
too far, when they exist only to justify the existence of a
line, civic spirit dies and there is no sense of community.
Canadian media, which could play an important role in
educating citizens, seem to be more interested in talking
about the wild life of Justin Bieber or Mayor Rob Ford
than about the number of homeless people on the streets
of Toronto or Vancouver.

I will not rehearse for my reader a hundred and one
reasons for or against Canada. Rather, I wanted to create a story that, like a tree whose life is contained in a
tiny seed, at each stage must grow into a new shape and
a new fruitfulness. My experiences in Iran, France, India,
and Canada taught me that a tree of life does not grow
at the same rate or with the same number of flowers and
leaves. There are times when autumn comes in the spring.

Now, I wonder how I could ever have come this far.
My short time in prison brought me international fame,

but that was a mixed blessing. At times, I was plunged into the depths of despair, feeling that I had been banished from life by the horror of a wild irrationality. At other times, I would feel sharp and vivid again and had surges of hope that the truth would triumph. Much to my surprise, when my so-called "confession" was broadcast on Iranian television, it had exactly the opposite effect from what the Iranian government had expected. People everywhere expressed their sympathy for my story and I was invited to give lectures around the world. I continued to teach at the University of Toronto with no prospect of a tenure-track position. However, my students were delighted to have a nonconformist instructor who initiated them into philosophical thought on nonviolence, Gandhian thought, and Iranian politics. I had hoped to teach Iranian politics either at the Munk School of Global Affairs or the Department of Near and Middle Eastern Civilizations but in both cases doors were closed to me by people who wanted to get mileage from my return to the University of Toronto but not to have modern and contemporary Iranian politics discussed and well-understood by students and academics.

I ended up taking a temporary position as associate professor with the Department of Political Science at York University, where I teach today. But even at York the same provincial mentality showed itself at my first meeting with an official at the University, who considered my references to my "friendship with the Dalai Lama" to be a form of "arrogance and bragging." But didn't critics of Hannah Arendt speak of her "arrogance" and her "tone of haughty superiority regarding things and men"? What is left of these critics today? Nothing. What is left of Arendt? Everything. I was happy to see some political science students at York taking interest in daily politics. But I wished that the pace of their readings in Marxism was as rapid as their discovery of the flattering signs that they might be a Che or a Rosa Luxembourg.

I also joined PEN Canada as a board member. This was the least I could do for other writers, intellectuals, and artists around the world who had been unjustly imprisoned. I became very active in the Iranian diaspora, writing, travelling, and giving lectures on nonviolence, forgiveness, and national reconciliation. It was during my second year in Toronto, in 2010, that I made the acquaintance of the Iranian-Canadian stage director Soheil Parsa and joined the board of his Modern Times Stage Company. Since then I have had the opportunity of participating in an intercultural artistic environment and learning a great deal from the constructive marginality of stage actors, dancers, and directors. My last intellectual collaboration with them was the preparation of a theatrical poem entitled "Forgiveness."

Inspired by the work of Václav Havel, whom I had met twice in Prague, and Nelson Mandela, one of my heroes, in 2012 I and a few friends in Toronto launched a new initiative to unite Iranians inside and outside Iran around a tolerant, nonviolent vision of the country's future. Our manifesto, Charter 91, so called because it was penned in the year 1391 in the Persian calendar, enshrines basic rights and rejects violence. It provides a blueprint for a future democratic Iran in which the rights of all minorities, including gays, are protected. It calls for freedom of assembly and freedom of speech, equality for women, freedom of religion, including the freedom both to convert and to be free from religion, an end to discrimination against ethnic minorities, and the abolition of capital punishment. Our aim in creating the charter was to use the intellectual freedom that we in the Iranian diaspora enjoy to provide all Iranians with the essential principles that must guide nonviolent change toward democracy. Many people inside and outside Iran signed the charter, and there were many lively debates about its contents.

Today, at the heart of my anxiety is knowing that my elderly mother, still in Iran, not only cannot see her granddaughter but is being pressed to pay my bail. This bail had originally been underwritten by my mother's and my wife's apartments in Tehran. But during a visit to Tehran in 2007, Azin, who is a shrewd businesswoman and a friend of the Rafsanjani family, found a way to free her apartment from this pledge, which left my mother to face the Iranian judiciary alone. However, now that I am a father, my priority is to protect my child. I think more and more about how to defend her, not so much from cuts and bruises or even life-threatening diseases as from mediocrity. The spread of conformism and mediocrity in the North American way of life has made the education of the next generation a difficult task. This is what the Iranian-Canadian community failed to grasp when I discussed with them the need to establish a Chair in Contemporary Iranian Politics at the University of Toronto. For most of the people I approached, among them many Iranian-Canadian builders and successful business people, it was far more important that their children make money than that they learn about the history and politics of Iran. I cannot hide my disappointment with the Iranian-Canadian community and the Canadian university system, but I don't think the struggle is over yet.

I feel about learning much as Gerald O'Hara felt about "the land" in *Gone with the Wind*: Learning is the only thing in the world worth working for, worth fighting for, worth dying for, because it is the only thing that lasts. Learning is worth more than money, than power, than fame. That is why I will never say never about returning to Iran to teach. I don't know if or when or how this will happen, but I know that I would go back if given the chance. Perhaps, like Dorothy in *The Wizard of Oz*, I should click my heels three times and say the magic words, "There's no place like home."

Epilogue

I HAVE NOW ARRIVED AT THE END OF THIS STORY, but I have no feeling that I have arrived at the end of my experiments in life. I have not ceased to grow inwardly and have not stopped learning from others. I have learned to continue seeking the truth and not to be content with ready-made answers. Philosophy taught me to be patient, but also to live passionately and wittily. It has beaten the drums of questioning into my ears in order to keep me awake and away from all dogmatic dreams. This has been my life up to this point. After living for more than half a century in several different cultures and societies, I have come to the conclusion that understanding other lives and learning from them is crucial to understanding and evaluating your own life. We think that our destinies are unique and yet they are the same. Perhaps it takes being in exile to fully comprehend this.

When Thomas Mann moved to New York in 1938 to escape the Nazi terror, he responded to a journalist's question upon his arrival by saying: "*Wo ich bin die ist deutsche Kultur*" (Wherever I am, there is German culture). Anyone who thinks and creates in exile, like Mann, has earned the right to say, "Wherever I create, there is human culture."

Those of us who live and write in exile cannot help but express our rootlessness. We have lost the rich, yet narrow, bond to a single place, and this allows us to be at home in any culture. I do not pretend to fit perfectly into any of the cultures in which I have lived, but I fit comfortably on the edge, in the margins, of each one by trying to keep a critical distance from all of them. Exiles are universal souls who live on the edge of an intercultural world, who celebrate the essential similarities between people everywhere, while paradoxically seeking to preserve whatever contributes to the creative ethos in each culture. The intercultural creativity of an exile generates not only new ideas but new models for a cosmopolitan citizenship. To live on the edge of your thinking, your culture, or your ego, as Paul Tillich suggests, means living with tension and movement. It fundamentally changes your identity. No longer frozen in a national character, your identity becomes more fluid and mobile, more susceptible to change, more open to variation. It is based not on belonging, which implies being owned by a culture, but on worldliness, on the negotiation of cultures and traditions of thought. In this sense, rootlessness is a precondition for building dialogue and peace. The exercise of thinking in exile is like standing at a crossroads. To think beyond suffering, exiles not only have to shake up entrenched concepts and categories but also to resist comfortable, familiar ethical and political categories, which turn us away from an intercultural and dialogical attitude.

My thinking about the world has always been tempered by the fact that life has no other goal than to live among others. The ability to think is the greatest gift humans have, but it comes into its own only among others. Only then can thinking freedom and the freedom of thinking unite. Losing freedom of thought does not make thinking freedom impossible. But there can be no real freedom without a life of the mind, because thinking makes life more exciting and makes us conscious of our capacity to be free.

Life would be ideal if we could achieve a balance between moral excellence and righteousness. And we need to pursue this ideal, whether the pursuit takes us along pleasant or painful paths. We pursue an ideal life of balanced choices and commitments, of a balance of passion and responsibility.

For me, the central concern of philosophy is the challenge posed by the idea of freedom and how it affects the social and political organization of a society. The centrality of this concern is revealed by examining the consequences of neglecting the issue of freedom. It goes without saying that freedom is the creative force behind philosophical thinking, just as philosophy contributes to the understanding and progress of the concept of freedom. Philosophers have tried to understand freedom as comprehensively and as critically as they can by making a contribution not only to its definition but to its realization. Hegel's statement that "No idea is so generally recognized as indefinite, ambiguous, and open to the greatest misconceptions (to which therefore it actually falls a victim) as the idea of freedom: none in common currency with so little appreciation of its meaning" is as true today as it was nearly two hundred years ago. Freedom is not only poorly understood but the word is also frequently misused.

The problem of freedom arises in every consideration of the nature of philosophical questioning itself. If the point of philosophical questioning is to elucidate the concept of freedom so that people can apply it, some account must be given of how most people no longer recognize freedom or take advantage of the possibilities it allows for creativity, as well as how it might be possible to correct this. In other words, philosophy is a way of thinking about the idea of freedom and its social and political applications, but also a way of thinking about the absence of freedom. Framing the problem of freedom and the problem of philosophical interrogation together points to the possibility that they are complementary parts of a more fundamental problem: how is human action or the human experience of politics shaped by the intertwining of philosophy and freedom?

Kant and Sartre maintain that our humanity resides in our freedom but, rather than simply accepting this, we first need to recognize that the political embodies permanent tension between philosophical interrogation and the institutionalization of freedom. To the extent that we are free to think, we can examine the process of thinking itself. We can, therefore, speak of freedom as philosophy's non-identical twin in the project of questioning and challenging what is thinkable and what is practised. Neither philosophy nor freedom could be taught or learnt once for all—both are unfinished projects of human history.

To be sure, someone who is already practising philosophical questioning cannot avoid the explicit and free interrogation of other modes of thinking and other forms of the thinkable. Philosophical questioning is a way of thinking that can create cracks in the surrounding walls of instituted thought. Smothering philosophical interrogation with theology goes hand in hand with the obliteration of freedom's creative and revolutionary nature. Philosophy as critical interrogation takes place in the gap between free instituting thought and instituted thought.

It is here that we can begin to understand why philosophy is the ongoing task of bringing freedom into political life as a corrective to the theological.

It is the civic task of philosophy to resist the very idea of a total theory of reality. To demand that the political organization of any society be founded on one total and complete theory is to declare politics non-thinkable and put an end to the freedom of thinking otherwise and anew. In other words, there cannot be a democratic society without democratic questioning, without civic questioning of the nature of democracy.

There is little point in talking and writing about philosophy without reflecting on the nature of philosophy itself. This is why the function of the civic philosopher, as a person who watches the inhumanities and injustices of the world (much of it in the name of philosophy), should be maintained, even if the concept today has lost its political strength. Philosophers cannot be replaced by tenure-track academics, even if the temper of the time suggests it. Philosophers still have much to contribute to the democratization of democracy. They will be useful to human societies as long as humans continue to believe that philosophy is not a futile word.

The civic task of philosophy today lies in the struggle between critical thinking and fanaticism. Whatever the price that philosophers may have to pay in the battle

against thoughtless tyrannies and hegemonic domina-
tions, we can still hope for the victory of inclusive, democratic thought. Searching for wisdom and safeguarding
it in times of crisis is the task that Socrates assigned to
the philosophers. He insisted that the philosopher is a
lover of wisdom and that the wise man is a man in pursuit of excellence. And it is the philosopher who has the
task of acting truthfully, righteously, and justly. In today's
globalized and technological world, where financial success and political power have become the highest values,
excellence is feared and unspoken. Attempting to achieve
it has become one of the great taboos of our society. Technology may be the modern religion of mankind, but not
everyone trusts its pseudo-certainties or derives happiness
from it. In *The Spirit of the Laws* Montesquieu noted, "The
political men of Greece who lived under popular government recognized no other force to sustain it than virtue.
Those of today speak to us only of manufacturing, com-
merce, finance, wealth, and even luxury." With the spread
of conformism and mediocrity in our world, the pursuit of
excellence has become a singularly singular task. Excellence
cannot be power, but it can offer us consolation—not in
the sense that it tells us life is good, for that would be a lie,
but in the sense that it teaches us the art of questioning
our certainties. As Seneca says, "Life's like a play: it's not
the length, but the excellence of the acting that matters."

ACKNOWLEDGEMENTS

ALBERT CAMUS ONCE SAID, "IN ORDER TO UNDER-stand the world, one has to turn away from it on occasion." Perhaps one can say the same thing about oneself. In order to understand one's own life, one must turn away from it. However, the deeper we go into ourselves, the more we see our own weaknesses. For a long period of time, I had difficulty writing about my life and my experiences in prison. It is not an easy task to write about oneself, especially when one has had to deal with difficult times. I went to bed with my nightmares, not being able to write about them. Then one day a friend of mine, Nojang Khatami, offered his support in the writing of my memoir. We talked things over and he offered his comments while assisting me with the editing. For that alone there will always be a piece of me indebted to him. I would also like to thank my friend and publisher, Bruce Walsh, for enabling me to publish this book. Bruce and

I worked together at PEN Canada. He is a pleasure to work with and I always appreciate his positive, collaborative, radical-minded, and high-energy work style. I would also like to thank Dinah Forbes, Joan McGilvray, Donna Grant, and Anne James for their help throughout the editing and proofreading process. Last, but not least: I beg forgiveness of all those who have been with me over the course of these past years and whose names I have failed to mention.

ABOUT THE AUTHOR

THE WINNER OF the Peace Prize from the United Nations in Spain and an advisory board member of PEN Canada, Ramin Jahanbegloo is an internationally celebrated philosopher and author whose books are published around the world. He is currently York-Noor Visiting Chair in Islamic Studies at York University in Toronto.

A NOTE ON THE TYPE

THIS BOOK IS SET IN ADOBE CASLON PRO, A variant of the work of William Caslon, and designed by Carol Twombly in 1990 for Adobe Systems. Caslon, who released his first typefaces in 1722, based his work on seventeenth-century Dutch old style designs, which were then used extensively in England. Because of their remarkable practicality, Caslon's designs met with instant success and became popular throughout Europe and the American colonies. For her Caslon revival, Twombly studied specimen pages printed by William Caslon between 1734 and 1770.

Text and cover design by Duncan Campbell, University of Regina Press.